THE
STORYTELLER

Growing Up in Clinton County, Ohio

by Pat Haley

For additional copies of The Storyteller: Growing Up in Clinton
County, Ohio, please contact:

Pat Haley
185 Woods Edge Court
Wilmington, Ohio 45177
937-205-7844
peh@cinci.rr.com

Cover and book design by Christina Murdock

Printed in the United States of America by:
Greyden Press, LLC
2251 Arbor Blvd.
Dayton, Ohio 45439

Dedication

I have been asked many times over the years how I am able to remember so many stories. I grew up in a family that loved sharing stories and handed them down from generation to generation. Like the story below, they stick in my mind.

Ten years ago, I was sitting in the Waynesboro, Virginia library when an interesting group of eight or nine elderly women marched through the front door. One must understand, Waynesboro still conveyed the feel of the 'Old South' particularly in behavior and manners.

The women conversed with each other inside a small room, separated only by a thin partition that allowed their voices to carry throughout most of the main floor of the library. They reminded me of the chatty character Aunt 'Pittypat' Hamilton, from *Gone with the Wind*.

My mind recalled a scene from the movie where Aunt Pittypat, always the southern belle, was helping the doctor in a makeshift hospital in Atlanta.

Dr. Meade: "Now you've got to listen to me! You must stay here!"

Aunt 'Pittypat' Hamilton: "Without a chaperone, Dr. Meade? It simply isn't done!"

Dr. Meade: "Good heavens, woman! This is a war, not a garden party!"

That dialogue quietly drifted through my mind as I heard the group of seventy to eighty year old women exchange stories. Although I wasn't eavesdropping, it was difficult to ignore their voices since each seemed to be talking louder as they competed for the group's attention.

"Martha, do you know I always thought that if Montgomery Cliff was with me for a night or two, I could change him?" I heard a woman say.

"He sure was handsome, wasn't he?" another woman answered. "You know, I felt the same way."

My wife, Brenda, son Greg and his wife Kristen, grandson Jack, my brothers Jim, Jack and Kevin, and my sister Rita, all love to tell stories. As did my parents, Bob and Ellen, and Grandpa Haley and Uncle Patsy.

I dedicate this book, *The Storyteller: Growing Up in Clinton County, Ohio*, to all of them, and to the people of Clinton County.

Acknowledgement

A special thank you to the following persons:

My wife, Brenda. I could never have completed this project without your continuous love and encouragement. Your input and your razor-sharp editing was invaluable.

My son, Greg. Your constant support was very meaningful to me, and your suggestions were always helpful and useful.

My brother, Jim. Your good humor inspired me to capture your whimsical side.

My brother, Jack. Your detailed recollections are priceless.

My sister, Rita. Your appreciation of family history and your sensitivity has encouraged me throughout this project.

Sam Stratman. Your Foreword is inspiring and sincerely appreciated.

And a very special thank you to Ms. Tina Murdock, whose expertise in graphic design brought this project to life.

Foreword

Since the dawn of recorded history, the story of humanity has been scratched into the surface of cave dwellings, shared around communal campfires, recorded in print and film, and saved digitally. Our instinct, it seems, demands that we remember our narrative and design new ways carrying on the tradition of sharing it with others.

We tell stories for every imaginable reason, but especially so that people may learn something about our deepest needs and desires. Storytelling is a method we employ to learn about our past and present. We have depended on storytelling to enlighten and inspire us about the vast potential of our lives, and to caution us about the limits of human frailty and imperfection. Stories become sentinels in our shared and uncertain future.

Author John Steinbeck once wrote that "a great lasting story is about everyone or it will not last. The strange and foreign is not interesting, only the deeply personal and familiar."

With this book, Pat Haley brings us the stories of his past, and ours' too. As you read, you may find yourself inspired, amused and enlightened by the many dramas and characters that unfold within these pages. You will experience moving stories of faith, hope, adversity and love.

This book is a testament to the fact that each of us live storied lives. By sharing the narratives of so many people that he has met along the path of his own journey through life, Pat has lifted a mirror before the reader. In doing so, he's hoping that we'll see a reflection of ourselves.

Sam Stratman

Table of Contents

THE
STORYTELLER

Introduction

"Just then, the train began to pass over a country road guarded by a railroad crossing with a gate adorned with bright red, flashing lights. Although it was dark outside, there was a full moon reflecting off the glistening snow. I could see the crossing arm fall across the tracks, and just then, I heard a bell on the crossing sign begin to ring. At that moment, I noticed a dirty old car parked next to the crossing arm. Sitting outside, on the front fenders of the automobile, were a man and a woman about sixty-years old and a young woman about eighteen. They were waving their hands and arms wildly to a faceless group of railroad cars speeding by, hoping for one last glimpse of their son and boyfriend."

This is a book of stories, and memories, as seen through my eyes, the fourth child of Robert and Ellen Haley.

Many of the stories you will find here I experienced while growing up in Clinton County, and supplemented by those experiences I have encountered during my travels through life.

My family is Irish, set apart because they are industrious people, who entertain others with their stories and whimsical outlook on life. It has been my good fortune to have observed these qualities first in my grandparents, then watched as the humor continued within the generation of my parents, aunts and uncles, and ultimately blossomed within my brothers and sister, son and now our grandson. I hope you enjoy my perspective, and may my memories trigger many of your own.

The Jimmy Stewart character, George Bailey, in *It's A Wonderful Life*, in a fit of anguish told his guardian angel Clarence, that he wished he had never been born. Unlike George, I am delighted to have been born into such a loving family and community.

To my gentle and religious parents, Bob and Ellen, and my siblings, Jim, Jack, Rita, and Kevin; I am grateful to have had the opportunity to join them in our home in Port William, Ohio.

I am fortunate to have had the opportunity to be touched by so many special people during my lifetime. I like to think the world is better in some small way because we all have been in it.

An Evening Train Traveling Somewhere in Pennsylvania

As he said, "Annie" I saw his face begin to crumble. The tears were now falling hard upon his cheeks

"**L**et's do something different this year," my wife said to me a few years ago, about three weeks before Thanksgiving. "Sure," I said. "What do you want to do?"

"Why don't we go Christmas shopping in Washington, D.C.?" she replied.

This would be one of our few Thanksgivings away from home. We would miss our traditional celebration and our families, of course; but we thought we could survive one year without the turkey, parades, and football. We decided we would be able give thanks wherever our travels took us.

A few days after Thanksgiving, Brenda and I were returning home aboard Amtrak's Lakeshore Limited after a few fun-filled days of shopping and sightseeing in our Nation's Capital. The snow was falling heavily, much like a picture from the Polar Express, or a scene from a Frank Capra movie. It felt good to sit back, relax, and watch the scenery pass as the train sped through Harper's Ferry, on to the flats of Maryland, and into the scenic river valley of Pennsylvania.

The Lakeshore Limited was especially enjoyable because the train contained a dome car; an elevated car wrapped in a wide expanse of glass. The seats in the dome car afforded an exceptional view of the snow that was gently falling upon the tracks, as well as, the upcoming railroad signals further down the road. It was fascinating to watch the twinkling lights of the houses in the country, and the red signals turn green as we passed under each switch spaced about a quarter of a mile apart. The dome car was crowded so I sat near the front listening to Christmas music and watching the miles go by.

As the music and thoughts flowed, a young man of about 18 years of age climbed the stairs to the dome car and asked if he could sit in the seat next to me. Since this was the only seat available, I said, "Sure, sit down."

As the young man took his seat, he was wearing a large cowboy hat that looked several sizes too big for his head, and a T-shirt emblazoned with "The University of Wyoming" on the front. The boy was talkative, and had walked in with a swagger. He told me he had just boarded the train at the previous station, a few miles back. As he continued to talk without a pause, I quietly removed my headphones. It was obvious the young man needed someone to listen. As we slid through the quiet countryside of Pennsylvania, the boy told me he was a Freshman student at the University of Wyoming, and was returning to school after spending Thanksgiving with his family. He said it would take a three-day train ride to return to college. I asked him if the trip was tiresome, and whether he would miss celebrating Christmas with his loved ones.

"No sir! Not me," he said. "I can handle this trip with no problem."

Then, like a scene from a movie, the boy suddenly caught sight of a small farmhouse sitting on a nearby hill overlooking the railroad tracks. As he pointed to the distance, he said with great enthusiasm, "That's my house!"

Then, as his home rapidly disappeared in the distance, I quietly asked him if he ever got homesick, being so far away at school?

"No," he said. "I love being away from home. In fact, I just broke-up with my girlfriend who I've known since first grade because she is just "too small town" for me. I outgrew her. I told her to find someone else, because I am going to date other girls in college."

Just then, the train began to pass over a country road guarded by a railroad crossing with a gate adorned with bright red, flashing lights. Although it was dark outside, there was a full moon reflecting off the glistening snow. I could see the crossing arm fall across the tracks, and just then, I heard a bell on the crossing sign begin to ring. At that moment, I noticed a dirty old car parked next to the crossing arm. Sitting outside, on the front fenders of the automobile, were a man and a woman about sixty-years old and a young woman about eighteen. They were waving their hands and arms wildly to a faceless group of railroad cars speeding by, hoping for one last glimpse of their son and boyfriend.

"That's my dad and mom," the young man shouted, "..... and Annie."

As he said the name, "Annie" I saw his face begin to crumble. The tears were now falling hard upon his cheeks, and the sobs began to shake his whole body. After composing himself, the young man left his seat quietly. I felt badly for him, as I placed my headphones back on my ears, and resumed listening to the soft sound of music. The mournful voice of Iris Dement was singing Our Town.

"Now I sit on the porch and watch the lightning-bugs fly.
But I can't see too good, I got tears in my eyes.
I'm leaving tomorrow but I don't wanna go.
I love you, my town, you'll always live in my soul."

Amid the most unlikely of circumstances, to the most unlikely of people, and for unknown reasons, once in awhile in this life we are allowed to comfort and, in some way, to lessen the pain and suffering of others; sometimes simply by listening.

Maybe that is what happened on a train, one cold snowy night after Thanksgiving somewhere in the mountains of Pennsylvania. And for those times, we are thankful.

When Talk Turns to Snow

Folks who had left their homes on Friday morning, found themselves stranded wherever they happened to be.

The heavy snow last week came like a thief in the night. In the courthouse, the subject quickly drifted from local government to snowstorms and blizzards. As the snowfall persisted and the winds howled around the crevices of the old windows, the County Commissioners shared a few snow stories before beginning the day's Session.

People naturally talk about snow in winter. Snow is a natural part of Ohio life, and has been since the glaciers passed through the Buckeye State more than two million years ago.

When the winds kick-up and the snow begins to blow, the stories usually focus on the back-to-back blizzards of 1977 and 1978. To those of a certain age, those are the major storms of their lifetime.

However, a few can remember another great winter snowstorm that once visited our community. It was one of Clinton County's most intense and extraordinary winter storms. According to the National Weather Service, this blizzard was one of the greatest windstorms on record. In fact, weather experts termed it an Extratropical Cyclone. My parents and their friends simply called it "The Snow of 50."

Our community awoke to lovely, falling snow on Friday morning, November 24, 1950. It was the day after Thanksgiving, children were out of school, and leftover turkey and trimmings were in most refrigerators. Children were sledding and building snowmen with their friends. However, the snow did not stop falling. It fell for days, piling-up higher than anyone had ever seen.

Folks who had left their homes on Friday morning, by the end of the day found themselves stranded wherever they happened to be. It brought almost everything to a standstill. Schools and businesses closed. Traffic stopped. The streets were deserted. Only the great steam locomotives were running. Some hardy fans had gone early to Columbus to watch the Ohio State - Michigan football game. Fortunately, they were able to catch a train at Columbus' old Union Station and detrained at the Pennsylvania Railroad stations in Sabina and Wilmington. Those fans who couldn't catch the trains, ended-up stranded in the deep drifts on the 3-C Highway, having to spend the night with kind-hearted farmers until the storm was over.

During the height of this terrible snowstorm, there was a young woman in the county who was ready to give birth and the nearest hospital was more than 30 miles away. Bear in mind this was before the arrival of Clinton Memorial Hospital.

One of the local farmers owned an old bulldozer with no cab or heating system. However, the townsfolk knew that the bulldozer was the only way they could get the woman to the hospital.

These good men lifted the young woman onto the seat of the bulldozer, wrapped her in a warm blanket, and started to the hospital.

The trip was beyond description by most accounts. Roads were snow and ice-covered and the wind whipped the snow into an angry, swirling, white monster. The arctic conditions were ferocious. The snow was higher than the fence posts, and in some areas, the wind had blown the snow into small mounds that made travel difficult even for the bulldozer. Incredibly, several men walked on foot, using scoop shovels accompanying the dozer. They battled 29-mile-per-hour gales that limited their movement. It took them 15 hours to transport the young woman to the hospital where she safely gave birth.

By the time the snow stopped falling on the following Tuesday, a record of 42 inches of snow had engulfed the region. Refrigerators were empty. Grocery supplies were running low. The only traffic moving along piled-high highways were the highway crews. Keeping in mind, at that time, there was no sophisticated snow removal equipment.

The three snowstorms in our lifetime all have something in common - a thread that binds them all together. As the snow flies, people in our community turn on the lights, strap on boots and emerge in heavy winter clothing. The garage doors go up and the front doors open. "Do you need help?" someone asks. Soon conversations begin and quickly the chatter turns to laughter.

We see neighbors we haven't seen in awhile. Everyone seems calmer, more relaxed somehow. The snow blowers appear. Children offer to shovel our sidewalks - for free. A good neighbor, Bart Powell, who gets up every morning before sunrise, even cleans away the snow from the windows of a neighbor's vehicle left parked outside overnight.

Before long, thermoses full of steaming coffee and hot chocolate appear. We stop thinking about the TV weather forecasters who are now in a state of frenzy. Soon, an almost festive atmosphere develops and we begin to build snow forts and snowmen. We throw a few snowballs at our wives and they throw them back at us. We go to Smith Place to sled ride.

Maybe a snowstorm once in awhile is not a bad thing after all.

A Hero Who Belonged to the Reds

Klu had to cut his uniform sleeves to allow his bulging muscles room to roam.

"**B**ailey gets what he wants and he turns it loose. It's hit in the air, shallow center field, going back is Phillips. Homer Bailey has pitched a no-hitter at 9:35 on this Friday night in Pittsburgh! And, oh yes, this one belongs to the Reds," With those words Marty Brennaman allowed us to catch our breath after nine innings of no-hit baseball by Reds pitcher, Homer Bailey.

Baseball is never far from our minds. After the no-hitter, my wife and I were talking about our favorite baseball players. Brenda likes Joey Votto. Homer Bailey is the favorite player of our grandson, Jack. I told a story about mine - Ted Kluszewski.

Theodore Bernard Kluszewski (Big Klu) spent 15 seasons in the Major Leagues, ten of them with the Cincinnati Reds from 1947 to 1957.

In 1957, Ted's last year with the Redlegs, my dad took me to Crosley Field to watch him play. Klu was not a weightlifter, but his arms were so huge that he had to cut his uniform sleeves to allow his bulging muscles room to roam. Or so the legend was told.

Those who remember Crosley Field will know the ballpark was an oasis, an island in the middle of an urban setting full of excitement and wonder. Inside the stadium, I remember the beautiful green grass, the bright lights, and the thrill of it all.

Crosley Field was located at the corner of Findlay Street and Western Avenue. When we arrived at the game, it was not uncommon for a neighborhood youth to ask my dad, "Would you like me to watch your hubcaps for a quarter?" It was a wise investment.

After Ted was traded to the Pittsburgh Pirates and then to the Chicago White Sox, every morning I looked up Klu's box score from the night before. I was always thrilled when he had hit a home run or went 2-for-4.

Years later as Sheriff, I had the opportunity to attend a Buckeye Sheriff's Association meeting in Cincinnati. In the midst of registering, I suddenly noticed Ted Kluszewski standing near a table, the guest of a uniform vendor.

I was nervous with anticipation as I approached Klu. Very rarely in life does one get the opportunity to meet their heroes. He stuck out his big hand. It enveloped mine like a baseball glove. Then, he said, "Pat, congratulations on the drug raid in Clinton County last week." I was taken aback. To this day, how he knew about the raid is still a mystery to me. I was aware that he lived in Warren County and perhaps he had read about it in the newspaper.

We talked baseball for several minutes. I told him how I had followed him in the newspapers throughout his career back in the 50s. He smiled and graciously said how much he appreciated my support. I'm sure Ted never gave any of the brief exchange a second thought, but I couldn't forget the unbelievable experience of my life, meeting my baseball hero, Ted Kluszewski.

Ted died in 1988. In 2003, before the inaugural game of the Great American Ball Park, the Reds dedicated a bronze statue of Ted on the plaza outside the main gate. I wanted to be there.

Unfortunately, I was unable to attend the dedication. I knew that when Klu's statue was unveiled on that momentous day, I wouldn't be thinking about long home runs or cut-out sleeves. Some remain heroes for different reasons.

I would be thinking about a simple handshake in a Cincinnati hotel some years ago, and the man they called Big Klu.

And All We Can Do is Remember

We all have special moments in life. Those moments that profoundly touch us, and come together because of circumstance or perhaps a coincidence of timing. Sadly, we can never repeat these times, for once they are gone, they are gone forever.

One such moment happened to me several years ago.

We had just buried my younger brother a few hours earlier. Leaving the cemetery, I was tired, emotionally drained, and faced a long, sad train trip back home to Staunton, Virginia.

My friend had dropped me off at Union Station in Cincinnati. As I entered the passenger waiting room at the Amtrak station, the stationmaster announced that my train would not arrive for another seven hours. I could call my friend, once again take advantage of his good nature, and spend another night at his home; or I could unpack my bags and try to fall asleep in the waiting room with the other passengers passing in the night. I decided to spend the night in the train station awaiting the 5:55 a.m. arrival of the eastbound train. And I am glad that I did.

As I began to prop-up my pillow, two things suddenly happened. The giant clock inside Union Station began to chime, and then I heard a trumpet sounding from inside the main corridor of the historic station.

I had never followed the music of the Big Band era, but I easily recognized the first few strains of Glenn Miller's song, "In the Mood." I quietly walked in their direction. Inside the beautiful and stately terminal, I observed an unanticipated celebration in full swing. The members of the orchestra, which included our own Rick Johnson of Wilmington, were dressed in tuxedoes.

Then, just beyond the orchestra were the soldiers, sailors, marines, and airmen along with their wives and girlfriends.

These military men were not the 20-year-old variety; but rather, 60-and 70-year-old veterans. Their uniforms were crisp, well tailored, and presumably just as they had been in 1945 when those same men likely walked through Union Station on their return home after World War II. In fact, that was the celebration. They were marking the 50th Anniversary of their return from the War.

For the longest time I sat near a stone pillar transfixed, watching from a distance. I was neither dressed properly nor worthy to intrude upon this private, hallowed celebration. Within minutes, the music began to slow and everyone rose to dance.

Earlier, I had noticed an elderly woman confined to a wheelchair, taking in the music and the excitement of the night. It was apparent she had suffered from a debilitating illness, perhaps a stroke; witnessed by her inability to move either her arms or her legs. As the gentle strains of the ballroom music began to fill the massive hall, the woman's husband, dressed in full military uniform, walked over to the wheelchair. The proud soldier bent down and carefully lifted his wife from the chair, her feet dangling, as she was unable to stand. Undaunted, her husband lovingly supported her as he placed her narrow arms around his neck and grabbed her around the waist to prevent her from falling.

Then, something even more unexpected and magical happened. Paralyzed and unable to initiate scarcely any body movement, she was able to move her mouth to form a smile; and as she did, one from the old soldier met hers. He held her tightly, and together they swayed back and forth on the dance floor for the longest time. I thought he would grow tired and return her to the wheelchair, but he kept her in his arms. They danced, although perhaps not as before, but the dance the pair now performed was one that everyone in the room, those of their same generation, completely understood. They were there for each other, with a love grown stronger over time. It did not matter that the years had robbed them of their youth and their vitality. Within them, I caught a glimpse of the inner strength, the loyalty, and the love of the generation that saved America over sixty-seven years ago.

President Ronald Reagan said of our veterans, "It is, in a way, an odd thing to honor those who died in defense of our country, in defense of us, in wars, far away. The imagination plays a trick.

We see these soldiers in our mind as old and wise. But most of them were boys when they died, and they gave up two lives, the one they were living, and the one they would have lived. When they died, they gave up their chance to be husbands and fathers and grandfathers. They gave up their chance to be revered old men. They gave up everything, for our country, for us. And all we can do, is remember."

Let us take time this coming week, on Veterans Day, to come together at the Veterans' Memorials in our small towns across America, and remember all who served in war and peacetime. To honor those who went to war, and those who never came home.

The Father and the Son

The best ice skater in town was Billy Stephens. It isn't an exaggeration to say he was extraordinary.

Yesterday, my wife, Brenda, and I retreated to our favorite chairs near the fireplace to enjoy an annual Christmas custom we began some years ago. We shared some of our Christmas memories, a ritual that has become a treasured time for us. As we talked, we easily began to slip back in time, to the memories that commonly take us back to family and friends, and to the good times we shared.

We spoke about Port William, and my growing up there. It would not be a stretch to say that Port William was very much like the fictional small town of Mayberry, North Carolina. If you can picture Andy, Barney, Helen and Thelma Lou ice-skating on a small pond in their little village, then you have an accurate picture of Port William in the 1950s.

As soon as the sun would set, it seemed as though the entire town, children and adults alike, would make their way down to Beam's Dam when Anderson's Fork froze over. Joe Beam would bring an old tractor tire down to the stream, and it did not take long before a large bonfire was started and lit up the sky.

The best ice skater in town was Billy Stephens. It isn't an exaggeration to say he was extraordinary. To us, his ice skating paralleled that of the Ice Capades. My brother, Jim, said Billy would push him on a small sled toward the dam, and Jim would close his eyes and hope Billy didn't slip and send Jim flying over the dam. At the last minute, Billy would turn Jim away from the dam, and the whole town would erupt in laughter.

There are times, however, when the world isn't filled with laughter and joy. We saw such a dark time two weeks ago in Connecticut. As we silently prayed for the families of the precious victims, our conversation naturally turned to God.

We talked about how we noticed even more Christmas lights coming on in our neighborhood after the terrible tragedy. We know the historic significance of candles, of course, and how they represent hope. Now, the brightly shining electric Christmas lights took on special meaning.

As we looked out the window, the lights seemed brighter than ever before. They were glistening as they symbolized our rejection of the darkness of violence and hate. Our neighbors were saying that the lights meant hope, happiness, and safety. One of my mother's favorite Bible verses was John 5.1. Quietly, Brenda recited from memory the passage, "And the light shineth in darkness, and the darkness did not comprehend it."

"I have one last Christmas story," I told Brenda. "Christmas is known as a time of love. Love of God and love of our fellow man. A few years ago, I saw it before Christmas at the YMCA in Staunton, Virginia."

The doors had opened early and loudly. It was exactly 6:20 a.m. A man and his father had entered the front door of the large building. The younger man was about 50-years-old and much larger than his dad. The older gentleman was in his late 70s. It was immediately apparent the younger man was a man of diminished mental capacity.

He walked with a slow and deliberate gait, shuffling into the building and up to the front desk where his father signed the sheet in order for the two of them to gain entry to the facility.

I had observed the pair many times over the last several months, watching the father help his son undress and assisting with dressing him in his gym clothes. After much effort, the father would guide his son through the locker room door past the people in the hallway, all the time never saying a word.

The younger man often talked loudly, laughing and teasing his dad. As they began their daily 15-minute workout, the older man would try to lift his son up the steps to the treadmill. The father computed the machine, placed his son's hands on the bars, and encouraged him to move his feet to the rhythm of the rolling belt.

I watched this ritual occur several times a week. It is without question, the father was very devoted to his son. He never grew impatient and always showed him kindness.

On this particular morning, I was jogging on the track when I noticed the two men coming down the stairs from the aerobic room. When they were about halfway down the stairway, something occurred that caught my eye. There was a commotion. The younger man turned and loudly cursed at his father, shaking his fist in his face, becoming profane and abusive. Everyone in the area turned and stared at them. The father calmly and quietly grasped his son's fist, and with much effort lowered his son's arm to his side. He continued carefully and tenderly to help his son down the stairs. The father never said a word.

To some, the elderly gentleman was suffering. That was not the case. It was clear that the loving father, with a caring heart, loved his son unconditionally, and that his son, who is disabled, was an extraordinary gift to his parents and to society. This father had proudly devoted his entire life to his son. He was never unkind or critical. It is similar to the love God has for his children.

"Brenda, do you think the young man knew God?" I asked. "He is disabled and may not have the intellectual capacity to turn his life over to God."

Psalm 116:6 says, "The Lord protects those of childlike faith. He did it for this man in Staunton, just as He did in Connecticut," she replied.

Blessed are the peacemakers: for they shall be called the children of God.

The Day the Boston Celtics Ate Hot Dogs in Cincinnati

They truly looked like giants. Even Cousy, a guard, seemed huge.

Some stories are just hard to believe. This is one of them. It is a story about the Boston Celtics, a professional basketball team in the NBA, and a boy and his dad. The two witnessed a delightful ten minutes many years ago, that remains frozen in time.

I know it is difficult to remember, but there was a time when professional athletes didn't make millions of dollars a year, but it's true. In fact, I read that Tony Lavelli, an early member of the Boston Celtics in the 1950s, even had a stipulation in his contract that the team would pay him an extra $125 a game to play his accordion at halftime. It was something the fans loved.

So, as the Astros, Falcons, Hurricane, and Wildcats are tipping-off their high school basketball seasons, we will take a few moments to remember a long-ago Sunday afternoon at the Cincinnati Gardens.

The journey began on a snowy Sunday as we headed south to Cincinnati in our family's 1955 Plymouth. It was the winter of 1958 when my sister, Rita, had asked our dad to take her to a cosmetology seminar in Cincinnati. Dad readily consented, not wanting Rita to drive alone the fifty miles in the snow that was falling that particular weekend. It was prior to the development of Interstate 71, and Route 22 and 3 was the only highway available to Cincinnati from Port William.

My dad asked if I wanted to ride along. I said sure. I was only ten-years-old at the time, but I had already been to several Cincinnati Reds games at old Crosley Field, so I knew the trip would be a long one. We made the journey without incident, and dropped Rita off at her meeting near Xavier University. Then, on our own, my father and I headed for a White Castle somewhere near the Cincinnati Gardens.

Now, it might certainly sound strange today, but at that time, eating at the White Castle was a treat because we never ate meals outside the home. Dad was sensitive to my mom's desire we eat healthy, nourishing meals at home; and they never patronized restaurants. However, since it was just the boys, it was okay this one time that we dine inside the small, cramped restaurant brimming with people. The urban atmosphere seemed so exotic to me.

When we had finished eating, my dad surprised me yet again. He asked me if I would like to see the Cincinnati Royals play. With no hesitation, I said, "sure." We just walked-up to the ticket booth and bought two tickets. I remember it like it was yesterday. The seats were excellent. I couldn't believe whom the Royals were playing on that particular day. The Boston Celtics. The Celtics were my favorite basketball team. I knew all of the players: Bob Cousy, Bill Sharman, Bill Russell, Sam Jones, K.C. Jones, Tom Heinshon, Frank Ramsey, and their coach, Arnold "Red" Auerbach. I was a big fan. Mom and Dad had even bought me green basketball shoes a few weeks before so I could emulate the Celtics.

I remember I was in awe as I watched the Celtics warm-up. We sat through the first half as the Celtics easily polished-off the Royals.

Then, the buzzer rang at half-time. My Dad and I walked from our seats to the concession area to get some hot dogs and drinks. You can imagine my surprise when I saw the tall men, extremely tall men, the professional basketball players standing in line just like everyone else. They very quietly and politely awaited their turn to buy the snacks. The men, larger than life, were wearing green short pants and basketball jerseys with "Celtics" emblazoned across the front in white letters. I couldn't believe my eyes! There they stood, Cousy, Russell, Ramsey, and a couple of other Celtics players were eating hot dogs and drinking Cokes during the half-time break. They truly looked like giants. Even Cousy, a guard, seemed huge.

I stood in awe as I watched the men quietly finish their drinks and head back to the locker room. There was unspoken courtesy and respect from the fans. The crowd never asked the players for autographs, or in any way disturbed them. The spectators inherently understood these were working people, taking a break from their jobs. In a strange kind of way, it seemed almost natural.

I have never recounted this story to many people. First, because most wouldn't believe me. Second, sometimes we just want to keep some memories for ourselves. There are days when the world seems to be swirling around me, and I need relaxation. It's then that I welcome the opportunity to take a few minutes for myself, and reflect back to this wonderful, unexpected experience - back over fifty years ago to that amazing spectacle from a simpler time and simpler place. It still brings a quick smile to my face after all of these years. The day the Celtics were eating hot dogs in Cincinnati.

Dave Cash Meets the Singing Ranger

On Thanksgiving Day, it has become a favorite tradition for my wife and me to call many of our friends that we've met during our travels and to wish them a 'Happy Thanksgiving'. This year, one of our most memorable chats was with Dave Cash, our elderly friend from Fishersville, Virginia. After spending some happy time catching-up, Dave asked me if I realized December 20, 2012 marked the thirteenth anniversary of the death of Clarence Eugene Snow. I said no, but Dave was quick to volunteer a story about Clarence. He said Clarence was born in the sleepy fishing village of Brooklyn, Queens County, on Nova Scotia's beautiful South Shore, just down the tracks from Liverpool, Canada.

"Do you know Clarence's stage name?" Dave asked.

"Sure, are you talking about Hank Snow?" I asked.

"Yes, indeed." He replied.

Dave went on to say Hank, widely known as

the "Singing Ranger", made his way to the United States in the late 1930s; bought a house in Madison, Tennessee; and named it the 'Rainbow Ranch' although it was a very modest home located in the center of an urban area. Hank never moved, and eventually died in that same house in 1999. Dave said Hank was quite a character, and an enterprising fellow. In fact, he was known to 'marry' many young couples he met on the road after he had enjoyed an adult beverage or two. Often, when a young couple would approach him at a performance or in a hotel, Hank would ask them if they were married. It they responded negatively, Hank would say, "Son, do you take this woman for your wife?" More often than not, the delighted young man would hand Hank a couple of dollars much to the bewilderment of the young woman.

As Dave warmed-up to the subject of Hank Snow, he shifted gears and said, "Let me tell you a story about Hank." Thoroughly engrossed by this time, I sat back in my easy chair as Dave recalled the first time he met Hank Snow.

"It was a summer evening in 1950. I was a young man working as a 'pin boy' at the Wayne Lanes Bowling Alley in Waynesboro, Virginia," Dave said. He went on to say that his boss, who also owned the Cavalier Theatre, always gave the kids who worked for him free passes to the theater. It happened to be that Dave was a big country music fan, and he knew that Hank Snow was going to perform at the theater on that particular night. Unfortunately, Dave didn't get to see the performance because he'd been working.

Hank was staying at the Esso Cabin Courts across the street from Nick's Royal Café, a Greek restaurant in town. After his shift ended that night, Dave said he walked to Nick's to get a hamburger. When he walked in, he saw Hank sitting at the counter. Dave sat down by Hank and struck-up a conversation. They continued the small talk for about 10 minutes, until Hank said he had to hit the road for his next singing engagement.

Dave asked Hank, "Mr. Snow, you don't happen to have any song books with you, do you?"

An amiable fellow, Hank said, "Sure, son, come with me. I have some in the trunk of my 49' Cadillac."

They walked out to Hank's car in the parking lot and Hank opened the trunk to a stack of books that were tied with twine string with a big knot on top of the bundle. Without a thought, all of a sudden Dave pulled out a big hunting knife to cut the string. Hank jumped back. He looked at Dave and said, "Son, what are doing carrying a big knife like that?"

Dave replied matter of factly, "You never know when you might need one around here!"

Hank proceeded to give Dave a picture and a program, autographed them both, before he began closing his trunk lid and moving on. Dave said he was thrilled.

More than thirty years later, in about 1984, Dave said he had the occasion to visit the Grand Ole Opry in Nashville, Tennessee.

While he was there, he said he had the opportunity to meet with Hank Snow again in person. Proudly, he recounted the iconic tale to Hank. Dave asked Hank if he remembered that night in Waynesboro in 1950.

Hank smiled and in his smooth baritone voice replied simply, "No, son, I don't, but that's a powerful story."

Singing
Christmas Carols

It warmed your heart, filled it, too, with melody that would last forever."

Lord St. John of Fawsley was a namedropper. A friend once said, "The trouble with you, Norman, is that you're such a compulsive name dropper."

"The Queen said exactly the same to me yesterday," came the rejoinder.

I know it may appear that I am namedropping, but really, I am not. I just thought I would reminiscence with you about a special moment that occurred a few years ago.

My wife and I lived in Staunton, Virginia for twelve years. Staunton is a picturesque town about the size of Xenia. It's nestled in the Shenandoah Valley, which stretches 200 miles from Harpers Ferry, West Virginia, in the north, to Roanoke in the south. Bordered to the east by the Skyline Drive and the Blue Ridge Mountains, and to the west by the Alleghany Mountains, the Valley is truly a beautiful part of the country.

Whenever we had the opportunity, we'd sit in our swing on the front porch of our home, since we had a perfect view of the Blue Ridge

Mountains at a distance. On most quiet pleasant nights, in our sleepy little neighborhood, we would observe many of our neighbors walking-by and more often than not, they would stop for a visit. In fact, it quickly became a bit of a neighborhood-gathering place, which we enjoyed.

On most evenings, if we sat there long enough, we would see many of our neighbors, Chuck and Annette, Susan and Colin, Don, Fred, and Susan and Louie. Joining them were Kitty and Al, Eliza, and an assortment of joggers, dog walkers, parents, and children, all walking on their way to unknown destinations.

Folks would see us sitting either on the swing or in the canopy-covered glider nearby, and would walk over and sit down to visit. We never had to issue an invitation, for they knew one was never necessary.

We became well-acquainted with one neighbor in particular, within a short period of time. We happened to be close in age, and for some reason, from the first day we talked, Don and I just sort of hit it off. He loved to talk about the 'old days' and was very nostalgic. One of those unexplainable things that happens to new friends sometimes. In just a matter of minutes, we realized we shared most of the same interests and many of the same memories. We liked the same type of people; the same type of music; we liked the same type of food, and the same type of old television shows. We even liked the same politicians.

As he once said, "We grew up with the same baseball heroes, the same musical heroes, and the same cowboy heroes even though we were hundreds of miles apart. We both recalled standing in line on Saturday mornings to watch Roy, Gene, Tex, and Lash LaRue at the Strand and at the Murphy Theatre respectively. Port William, Ohio was a long way from Staunton, Virginia. But, I guess really, only in miles."

One year as Christmas approached, my wife and I began making our plans to return to Ohio, as we always did, to celebrate the holidays with our friends and family. However, as Christmas drew near, I realized my vacation leave had expired, and had no time off other than Christmas Day. I would be stuck in Staunton by myself on Christmas. Christmas was just a few days away when my friend, Don, casually asked me when we were heading to Ohio for the holidays. I told him I would be spending Christmas in Staunton due to my work schedule. "Why don't you come over to the house on Christmas Eve and spend the evening with us," he asked. "All the family will be there, and they would enjoy seeing you, too."

Although I appreciated his kindness, I told him I couldn't impose on him and his family on this most special holiday. He insisted and I finally relented. We had a delightful evening at his home with much talk, laughter, and food. After the reminiscing and sharing of memories began to wind down, they called us into the den and began to gather around the piano. My friend, Don Reid, walked over to his brother, Harold, and asked him and their good friend, Phil Balsley, to join him in singing some special Christmas songs.

Some may not recognize the names, but these were the Statler Brothers. Words cannot describe the surreal feeling I had listening to the blended harmony of the Statler Brothers singing Christmas Carols in the living room of their home on that snowy and blessed Christmas.

As author Bess Aldrich said, "Christmas Eve was a night of song that wrapped itself about you like a shawl. But it warmed more than your body. It warmed your heart, filled it, too, with melody that would last forever."

Let's Save the Wilmington Drive-In

The aroma of popcorn, hot dogs and hamburgers filled the summer air as night settles in and the screen came alive.

As I glanced out the window at the beautiful snow the other day, my thoughts drifted back to the year that has just passed into history, and to the Top Story List of 2012 written by Ms. Andrea Chaffin of the Wilmington News Journal. Andrea had written about football championships, a local hero, politics, people who wanted more money, and a story that stopped me cold – the closing and uncertain future of the Wilmington Drive-In Theatre.

This story news was of particular interest to me because the Chakeres Wilmington Drive-In Theatre and I have something very special in common. We both were born in Clinton County in the summer of 1948. My mom gave birth to me in our home in Port William, and just eight miles down the road on State Route 134, the Chakeres family gave birth to what has become one of the great landmarks in Clinton County.

As many did back then, my parents loved movies on the big screen. Mom would pack baloney, potato chips, cupcakes, Barq's root beer, and off we would go. We watched John Wayne, Randolph Scott, Joel McCrea, and Audie Murphy riding across the silver screen almost every weekend during the summertime.

It seemed many parents wanted their babies to grow-up to be cowboys. A Port William neighbor of ours, Raymond 'Steamboat' Hughes, loved Westerns, too. 'Steamboat' had a little cart he pulled behind his car, and often filled it with neighborhood kids he took to the Drive-In on Friday nights. My brothers told me a classmate of theirs had purchased an old funeral home limousine and every weekend it would be filled, including the trunk, with boys from Port William. Mr. Bill Reisinger, Manager of the Drive-In, would see them coming and wave them in. "I guess they need to come to the Drive-In pretty bad," he joked.

My parents would arrive as soon as the gates opened, usually while the sun was still shining brightly. The Drive-In had a playground in front of the screen, with swings, slides and a merry-go-around. As kids, we often played until dark. Then, my dad would flash the car lights and we knew it was time for the movie to begin, and to return to the car. We never failed to linger just a bit to catch a few lightning bugs on the way to our back seats.

There was no better place in Clinton County to be on a Friday night than the Drive-In. Where else could you watch two movies, sometimes three, for less than a dollar? Most of our neighbors were there, and the Drive-In was safe. The sound of tires slowly crossing the gravel was a sound like no other. Parents were aware that children were present, and the wheels were barely turning prior to pulling into the grassy area beside the speakers.

A certain smell could be found only at the Drive-In. The aromas of popcorn, hot dogs, and hamburgers filled the summer air as night settled-in and the screen came alive.

Two of my classmates and friends, Joe Spicer and Larry Baker, worked at the Drive-In. Recently, I spoke to Joe and asked if he had any stories about the Drive-In he cared to share. "None fit to print in a family newspaper!" he laughed. We reminisced about some of our friends who had worked at the Drive-In, and Tom (Tink) Ryan's name quickly came to mind. Tom was a fixture at both the Drive-In and the Murphy Theatre for many years.

"Do you remember a game called Mr. Spotty that was played at intermission?" Joe asked. In the 1950s, many cars came equipped with spotlights much like those found on police cruisers. A small graphic was flashed on the screen and patrons were expected to follow the jumping and bouncing Mr. Spotty with their spotlights. Mr. Spotty was a source of great amusement, as car lights lit up the northern part of Wilmington. Some even used the excuse of Mr. Spotty to 'accidentally' shine their lights into the steamy cars around them. I remember Mom saying to Dad, "Oh, Bob. Don't do that. They might have children asleep."

A prize was given at the end of Mr. Spotty, and just to be funny, many of the drivers would honk their horns. Mr. Reisinger, who was considered one of the nicest men in town, would get on the car speakers and tell the drivers to quit blowing their horns. "Babies are asleep in the cars. Have some consideration!" he would announce.

The Drive-In was also a good place to take a date. My older

brother, Jim, once said, "High school boys liked taking their dates to the Drive-In and sitting in the back row." He never elaborated, quickly changing the subject.

When I was in high school, I remember my mom asking me one evening why I enjoyed taking dates to the Drive-In so much. "I just love movies, I guess," I said. Then, for some reason I smiled.

"Why are you smiling?" Mom questioned, with a serious look on her face.

Today, a typical response might be, "What happens at the Drive-In stays at the Drive-In." However, I wasn't that brave. In those days, parents still believed in corporal punishment. I replied simply, "Oh, no special reason." Like my brother, I tried to change the subject.

There are certain landmarks a community needs to keep. As someone aptly said, "Saving the past enriches the present." The Murphy Theatre is still with us because of the dedication and hard work of our community to save it. Is it possible we can we do the same for the Wilmington Drive-In Theatre? How nice it would be to hear the words of Mr. Reisinger once again, "Thank you for visiting the Drive-In. We hope you will come again."

Dreaming of a Dead Man Downtown

Forgiving our own failings is an important act of releasing one's self from the past.

Have you ever had an unsettling dream - one that seemed so real it took time to realize it actually was a dream? I do not dream often, but when I do, my dreams usually occur just before I awake in the morning. For whatever reason, a couple of years ago, just before I took office as county commissioner, I had such a dream.

In my dream, there was a man, a longtime owner of a local business and known by many, who had died several years ago. I dreamt I was walking near his business, and I saw him sitting in his customary chair in the back of the store working on a project. Surprised to see him sitting there, uncharacteristically, I rushed into the store and blurted out, "I thought you had died!"

"I did," he replied.

"Well then, what are you doing here?" I asked.

"I get to come back from time to time to visit," he said.

"I'm glad to see you, but I didn't know you would be allowed to return to earth. I bet you are really enjoying Heaven," I told him.

The man slowly shook his head. "I didn't get into Heaven," he sadly stated. "I am in Hell." I was absolutely dumbfounded by his comments.

"I cannot believe you, of all people, are not in Heaven. Why? What happened?" I asked.

"Let me tell you," he continued. "I was as surprised as anyone. When I died, I figured I had a lock on Heaven, but boy, was I disappointed," he said, with tears welling-up in his eyes. "I always thought Heaven would be full of people, but I was wrong. Few people get into Heaven, because many of us at some point in our lives have turned our backs on God, and have never truly repented," the man said. "What we have been told about (many being called, but few being chosen) is truly accurate," he said. "God really means what he says. My heart is broken," he went on.

I was deeply bewildered. Thinking aloud I broke the silence. "I just cannot believe you didn't get into Heaven. If you didn't qualify, I can't imagine many others who would either."

I had always known the man to be a kind and gentle soul, whom I thought had lived a good and honorable life.

"What are things like in Hell?" I asked him, pressing the point.

He took a deep breath and said, "I was surprised. At first, it wasn't so bad. We were given pizza once in awhile; and as you can see, I get to visit folks at home now and then. The biggest problem is the isolation from God and the sadness. I am so disheartened, because I leaned on God in times of trial during my time on earth. As time goes on, I am becoming increasingly scared, because I'm afraid Hell is continuing to get worse and it is affecting me. I have noticed more and more that negative feelings and reactions are welling-up inside me," he said. "And I believe they are just the tip of the iceberg. I encourage you to think, and if there is sin in your life, confess and repent. Don't end up like me," he concluded.

Then, abruptly I awoke from my sleep. I felt a deep sense of foreboding and my breathing was heavy.

It was only a dream, I thought to myself. Thankfully. Yet, throughout the rest of the day those thoughts continued to linger in my mind.

I thought back. Why was this particular man, who was such an unlikely participant, the source of the dream? For although I had always appreciated his easy manner and pleasant personality, he and I had never developed a close, personal relationship.

In the early hours of the morning, a number of other questions surfaced in my mind relating to the dream. One can only surmise the answers. This is commonly what happens with dreams. They are open to interpretation. One interpreter of dreams said, "Dreaming of Hell suggests that you are experiencing self-awareness, recognizing the need to become more responsible, and undergoing a period of change."

That may be true, because recently I have sensed change within me. There is more calmness and a stronger acceptance of life's twists and turns. Although forgiving ourselves can be much harder than forgiving others, forgiving our own failings is an important act of releasing one's self from the past.

However, as each of us has an opportunity to reflect upon our lives, we recognize the choices and the decisions we have made, both good and bad, are part of our being. We know they have each shaped us, and have helped make us who we are today. We learn from them, and we move forward with greater knowledge and understanding of who we are.

I understand few of us get a second chance in life. However, those of us who do, feel a great sense of redemption. "Enter through the narrow gate. For wide is the gate and broad is the road that leads to destruction, and many enter through it. But small is the gate and narrow the road that leads to life and only a few find it."

With those words, my mind took me back to my dream and to the cautionary words from the dead man downtown.

Just Arch Your Back and Purr

Invited to stay as a guest at Andy's home, Mr. Tucker became very nervous and irritable.

The small town was about the same size of Wilmington. The economy had been in crisis for several years since the textile mills and furniture factories left town for China. The Blue Ridge Foothills, which run north from North Carolina, into Virginia, and past our former home in Staunton, were visible in the distance. There were big box stores on the outer corporations, but to our surprise and delight, the downtown was booming.

As we entered Mt. Airy, North Carolina, we knew we had entered a special place. Lifting like the black-and-white life of Kansas when first entering the bright, colorful Land of Oz, our eyes grew wide as we passed Opie's Candy Store, Floyd's City Barber Shop, and Wally's Service Station. Across the street, we saw a couple of men sitting on courthouse benches.

There were maple and sycamore trees lining the streets just as we had pictured. We saw the flags honoring patriotism and could sense the small town values. We were in Andy Griffith's hometown.

After more than fifty years, the Andy Griffith Show is still popular. Mayberry is a frequent imaginary destination for those us who enjoy returning to the ageless comfort of this innocent time and special destination. The world of Andy, Barney, and Floyd, holds a special place in our hearts.

Our son, Greg, began to watch the reruns of the Andy Griffith Show during his high school years. Greg recently said he has seen each of the 249 episodes of the show. Several years ago, Greg founded the Andy Griffith Show Rerun Watchers Chapter in Clinton County. In order to become a member in good standing, a chapter must be named after one of the characters, or from a phrase from the dialogue in the series.

In the episode entitled, The Bookie Barber, Andy was sitting in the barber chair having his hair cut by Floyd Lawson, the eccentric barber. Two men wearing black suits and black hats entered the barbershop. The two men pretended they were barbers who wanted to go into business with Floyd, when actuality they were bookies who wanted to cover their suspicious scheme with the pretense of a legitimate business. The men encouraged Floyd to allow them the opportunity to fulfill Floyd's lifelong dream of owning a two-chair shop. Floyd played right into their hands. Although Andy was suspicious, he good-naturedly told the men how Floyd had started barbering by cutting the hair on cats when he was just a little boy. "Sometimes Floyd forgets he is not cutting cat hair, "Andy said. "Once, when I became a little fidgety, he suddenly reached down and began to scratch my back. You don't even have to pay him if you just arch your back and purr," he continued.

This amusing phrase gave Greg the name for his chapter.

Why is the Andy Griffith Show still so popular after all of these years? Many believe the answer is because people want to identify with the goodness of Mayberry and its' citizens. In this age of daily crisis, Mayberry represents an innocent, simpler time. It makes us feel young again.

Change came slow to Mayberry. Seldom was anyone in a hurry, with the exception of Malcolm Tucker. Mr. Tucker was a principle figure in one of our favorite episodes entitled, Man in a Hurry.

Mr. Tucker, an important businessperson, was enroute to Charlotte when his car broke down just outside Mayberry. He walked into town on a very hot day, and demanded that the mechanic, Gomer Pyle, fix his car immediately. Gomer told him he couldn't fix the car because it was Sunday. He said Mr. Tucker would have to wait until Monday. In the meantime, Mr. Tucker waited impatiently for the time to pass. Invited to stay as a guest at Andy's home, Mr. Tucker became very nervous and irritable. He was unwilling to sit down with Andy and Barney for a Sunday chicken dinner. Mr. Tucker continued to fret, later walking out onto the front porch where Andy was playing his guitar. Andy and Barney began to sing "The Church in the Wildwood" in perfect two-part harmony. The singing and easy camaraderie of Andy and Barney slowly begin to soften Mr. Tucker. He began quietly to sing along with Andy and Barney. You could see him revisiting his childhood as he sang each verse louder and with more enthusiasm.

The Man in a Hurry episode does for our children now what it did for us in the Sixties. It provides us the opportunity to escape this careless world for thirty minutes, into a bygone era of simplicity. We love to join Andy and Barney on the front porch after a big Sunday dinner as they decide who should go down to the corner drug store and buy ice cream. It reminds us of the values many of us wish were prevalent today. Many people seek their own Mayberry. The magic of electronics allows us to visit the delightful town anytime we desire. With the push of a button, Greg and I enter this magical community, sit back, pour some lemonade, and "just arch our backs and purr."

Bogie Visits Sycamore Glen

Sometimes words aren't necessary. Sometimes it's just enough to be together to help the worry of the world fade away.

Tomorrow is Valentine's Day. My wife, Brenda, and I have plans to begin our evening with a quiet candlelight dinner. We will share with each other those special thoughts, those heartfelt feelings, and speak of things that warm our hearts and souls.

We will talk about the good times. We will easily remember our trip to Harper's Ferry when we walked for an hour in the rain, and bought ice cream in the little country store.

We might speak of our night on Broadway in New York City on New Year's Eve, when we ate at the little neighborhood delicatessen. We will recall the time we sat on the lawn of the U.S. Capital to hear the United States Marine Band play the spellbinding concert on the Fourth of July.

We might laugh about the time Brenda, who is a 'hugger,' was serving as an usher at a major fundraiser for a former U.S. presidential candidate. I forewarned her. Do not try to give him a hug when he passed by her to reach his seat.

Then we might ask, sadly, "Do you remember

the time we attended a concert by a famous singer and we saw him cry as he sang a love song?" We learned the following day that his wife of thirty years had just filed for divorce.

Moving on to more pleasant thoughts, we will laugh, because laughter binds us together. A few years ago we recall our neighbors in Staunton, Virginia entrusting the care of their prized toy poodle, 'Lucky', with us while they traveled. "We never worry when 'Lucky' stays with you," they said. "We know you would never let anything happen to our little guy." We never had the heart to tell them that earlier that morning 'Lucky' had jumped out of our car window as we left the downtown area. Thankfully, he was okay.

We might then recall the time our own little poodle, 'Doc', though uninvited showed-up at our neighbor's outdoor wedding. When we located him, the caterer smiled as he told us Doc had eaten all of the deviled eggs when the chef had turned his back in the kitchen.

Our conversation will drift back to all the times we've stood strong for each other, at funerals, during those long hours of surgery, and more. We will talk about how we left a place we loved in Virginia to return home to family and friends.

We're likely to reminisce about the loss of our dear pets over the years, and how we spent the nights beside the fire talking about the pleasure they've brought us. We will talk about the times when we stood together when the politics went sour, or maybe just those nights when we needed someone to listen when our hearts were breaking.

Sometimes words aren't necessary. Sometimes it's just enough to be together to help the worry of the world fade away. Sometimes we just need to say we are sorry.

Brenda will say she remembers the special Valentine's Day performance many years ago with Richard Harris in Camelot. He sang a song that night that I sometimes sing to her. She never complains that my singing is off-key or flat.

The song begins, "How to handle a woman? There's a way, said the wise old man. A way known by every woman since the whole rigmarole began. Do I brood or play the gay romancer? Said he smiling, No indeed. Mark me well, I will tell you, Sir: The way to handle a woman is to love her. Simply love her."

Yes, Brenda and I will enjoy reflecting on the passing years recalling our special memories of those years together. We know life is short. Life is not without trials, and the past year has given us a few crosses to bear.

In closing, at the risk of sounding cliché, there are no words to express the words of appreciation due my wife. She has stood strong beside me during the most difficult times. We each have been on both sides of victory, and we can always count on being there for each other. We lock those moments tightly inside our hearts.

As our Valentine's Day winds down, that evening we will watch Humphrey Bogart and Claude Rains in the movie, *Casablanca*. Quietly watching as they walk-off into the mist and fog at the airport and Bogart says, "Louie, I think this is the beginning of a beautiful friendship."

I know that feeling well. Brenda is my very best friend.

The Man Who Loved Beets and Internet Dating

News traveled fast, so he found himself with neighbors who wouldn't socialize with him.

This isn't a deep analytical story. It is simply a little slice of life.

Our neighbor, who we will call 'Frank', was a man quite different from those who came before him to our laid-back neighborhood in Staunton, Virginia. Frank was 75-years-old, free-spirited, and lonely. A man with time on his hands, he had two unlikely passions in life: beets and Internet dating. He said he had recently taken-up beet eating for nutritional purposes. His obsession with Internet dating was longer standing, and had taken him all over the East Coast to meet like-minded women.

Frank was a man who loved to discuss the attributes of Internet dating - anytime and every time he engaged a neighbor in conversation. Twice divorced, some might call him 'unlucky in love'. He informed us that his new dentist had "fired" him as a patient, and that the local YMCA banned him, on both occasions for inappropriate behavior.

Before long, Frank began a practice of walking

down the sidewalk in shorts, no shoes, offering whatever he had cooked for dinner (usually beets) to the neighbors, which was a bit unorthodox for the locals. Needless to say, some were a bit frightened of Frank. News traveled fast so he found himself with neighbors who wouldn't socialize with him. At least not many.

It was early spring, and as they say, love was in the air. Frank stopped by to visit telling Brenda and me that he was planning a trip to South Carolina to meet a woman from Florida he had chatted with on the Internet. He told us the city they had selected was halfway between Staunton and where his new friend lived in Florida. In the weeks leading-up to the planned rendezvous, Frank stopped by our house every time he saw us in the yard. Each time he visited, his anticipation was mounting. He could hardly wait for the meeting. Finally, the big day came and he was off to meet his new friend. No doubt, we had concerns.

We heard nothing from Frank until the following weekend. While working in our yard, he approached, and sat down to talk. In true approach-avoidance fashion, we asked him how his trip to South Carolina had gone. We weren't quite prepared for what we heard next.

"She was a very nice woman, full of fun and spirit. We had an excellent dinner. I, of course, had beets," Frank began.

"Then, the lady said she didn't like beets," Frank said. "I was flabbergasted, and didn't know what to say. For some reason, I told the woman that I felt like I had just lost my mojo! Wasn't that a ridiculous thing to say?" he asked.

Brenda and I quietly looked at each other.

Frank continued with his story. "The woman said she was not sure what mojo meant, and she was going back to her room. She also mentioned she would be leaving early the next morning to go back to her home in Florida."

"Please do not contact me again," she added.

"That pretty much ended our date, "Frank said.

Frank said the unhappy ending had shaken him. Back in his room, it was some time before he settled down enough to become sleepy.

"All was going well until about 1 o'clock in the morning," Frank stated. He said he had awakened and arose to go to the bathroom.

"All of a sudden, I passed what I deemed to be blood," Frank said. As any person would be, he said he was startled. Fearing he might have been hemorrhaging, he said he quickly called the front desk who sent the night clerk up to his room. As soon as the clerk entered the room, she screamed. Frank said, "Then I screamed!" With those words, Brenda and I dropped our yard work to listen to the unfolding story.

"With no time to waste, instead of waiting for an ambulance, the night clerk rushed me to the local Emergency Room where a battery of tests was run," Frank said.

After more than thirty minutes, gripped with dread and fearing the worst, Frank said the Emergency Room doctor returned to his room and pulled-up a chair next to the gurney. As the doctor closed the drapes around Frank's bed, excited to learn the diagnosis, Frank blurted out, "Quick, Doctor, what's wrong with me? Why am I passing all of this blood? How bad is it?"

Composed, and slightly amused, the doctor took a long look at his patient. He then asked the question, "Frank, have you by chance been eating beets?"

"Why, yes, doctor. I had a lovely meal of beets earlier this evening," Frank anxiously replied. "Why?"

"Well, the tests are conclusive," the doctor said. "You will be fine. That's not blood, Frank. That's beet juice!"

And with that, Frank's obsession with beets was over. Thankfully, we were quietly relieved, as any good neighbors would be.

A Mother's Love

Mom was the person our neighbors came to when things weren't going right in their lives.

I am a private man who lives a very public life. This story is personal, but I wanted to honor, in some small way, my mother, Ellen Haley, who died twenty-eight years ago yesterday.

I remember the call. "Your mother is ill. We are taking her to the hospital," my dad said quietly over the telephone.

For several years Mom's health had been declining. Although her bodily aches and pains were coming more often, she hadn't been feeling terribly bad. We all knew she just hadn't been feeling as good as normal, and certainly not as well as we had wished she would.

Arriving at the hospital, I was pleased to find Mom sitting up in bed, alert. When she saw me, she became animated saying, "Hi, Pat," softly smiling as she said the words. "How are you?" she asked.

"I am fine," I responded. "How are you feeling?" I asked her.

"Pat, I am dying, you know," she said quietly. Her voice was peaceful as she uttered the words.

I looked at my mother, heartbroken. It was difficult to comprehend the depth of her medical condition, and how within the last few hours so much had changed. She lay back on the pillow and closed her eyes to rest. I closed my eyes, too.

My mind drifted back to my 'growing up' years. I thought of my parents, and my brothers and sister, Jim, Jack, Rita, and Kevin. I reflected on the memories from our little town. I thought of the times we drove past the cornfields, past the tiny school, Beam's Mill, and the dam. Our family knew everyone in town. And they knew us.

Our parents, Bob and Ellen, defined us.

Beginning in the first grade, my mom signed a permission slip that allowed me to walk home from school for lunch. She wanted me to have a nutritious meal each day at noon. I can remember walking into the house and smelling the aroma of my favorite meal slowly cooking; Swiss steak and usually a potato baking in the oven.

Mom was the person our neighbors came to when things weren't going right in their lives. She served many roles in our community including wedding planner, confessor, and marriage counselor before we needed names for such things. Many young brides in Port William in the 40s, 50s and 60s served wedding cakes baked by my mother at their weddings.

Men down on their luck stopped at our house. They knew my mother would give them a meal and some money to help them on their way. Once, a local farmer and his family lost their home in a fire. Mom invited them to stay with us. They stayed for a few weeks until they were back on their feet.

Mom was Port William's Bureau of Motor Vehicles Deputy Registrar. People from throughout Clinton County came to our house to buy their licenses because, in their words, my mother "was always so nice to them."

As we entered our teenage years, mom was normally awake when we returned home from a date or a ball game. Then she would rest, knowing we were safe.

My mother loved picnics. She enjoyed cooking us hamburgers and fried potatoes at the Wilmington City Park under the shelter house, and sometimes at the roadside parks in Cuba, Martinsville, or Blanchester. We loved the smell of burning wood as we waited on dinner, cooking over open fires.

Good manners were important to my mom. They became important to her kids, too. She gave to us what her parents had given to her.

Just then, the noise of the doctors administrating medication to ease her pain brought my mind back to the present, those many years ago. All of us stood beside her. We watched, knowing there was little we could do. Nevertheless, we wanted to be with her, as she had been there for us throughout our lives.

Within a few moments, the doctor simply said, "Your mother's heart has given out." I thought to myself, a heart that had worked hard all her life. Mom's was a heart full of love, and a heart that she openly shared with others. She truly was an outstanding woman.

Our hearts ached, but her memory salved the sadness. We treated our mother with the same respect she had given us all of our lives. We all tried to give back to her the politeness, the courtesy and the love she had given us in abundance.

The death of my mother changed my life. Those of us of who have lost our mothers know the feeling well. There is a void never filled.

We do go on. We are just never the same.

The Day We Looked Into the Soul of the Left Fielder

The man on the radio said the Cincinnati Reds begin Spring Training in the lovely desert town of Goodyear, Arizona in twenty days.

Our son, Greg, is one of the biggest Reds fans in Lexington, Kentucky. On most summer nights when the Kentucky moon is beginning to peek its head through the evening sky, and shortly after the birds have gone to bed for the night, Greg and his wife, Kristen, pull up chairs on the patio, and turn on the radio. They sit back and listen to Marty Brennaman and his sidekick, 'The Cowboy,' once again bring Reds baseball to life.

Greg called the other evening after dinner, and we began our ritual of talking about the Reds and baseball in general. The snow was beginning to fall slowly against our windows, and a nice fire was glowing in the fireplace. It was a great time to reminisce. He asked if I remembered the boy playing left field. Those words were all it took to transport us back to a delightful afternoon some years ago near the hometown of Bob Evans.

Greg was nearing completion of his sophomore

year at Rio Grande University. I had arrived at 'Rio' early on a Friday afternoon to drive him home for the weekend. We had some time to kill before heading home, and decided to explore some of the local hangouts. We had traveled just three miles when we came upon Centerville. The hamlet was a speck on the map; a crossroad much like its neighbors Kerr and Patriot. We saw a sign that said, "Population 103." At the intersection sat three older homes, a corner grocery, and a baseball diamond.

We were delighted to discover a softball game in progress, and decided to stop and watch on that warm, lazy afternoon. As we settled into the game, we nonchalantly leaned against the outfield fence. The young man playing left field turned around and spoke without any urging from us.

He blurted out, "I'm not very good."

Greg and I looked at each other in surprise, wondering first, why the young man would make such a statement in the middle of a ball game, and secondly, why he would initiate it with two perfect strangers. We soon found out the left fielder wasn't finished with his observations.

"I have a weak throwing arm, and I'm not very quick," he continued. "In fact, I don't know why they even have me on the team."

After that comment, we knew there was going to be more at play in the game beside the softball.

"I bet you're a good hitter though," I said, as I found myself trying to encourage the young stranger.

"Can't hit a lick," he responded.

Just then, a sharp crack of the bat notified us that a softball was heading our way, and progressing in a hurry. True to his prediction, the left fielder dropped the ball.

"Throw the ball to second base! Cut him off," we yelled, as we began rooting for the young ballplayer.

After the play was complete, we began 'coaching' the left fielder. We suggested he think ahead and plan his strategy in case they hit the ball in his direction.

Suddenly, a batter hit a screaming line drive his way at a tremendous rate of speed.

"Charge the ball as fast as you can and throw it directly to third," Greg reminded the left fielder. For some unknown reason, we felt we had to give the young man, whom we had never seen before in our lives, a generous dose of self-confidence.

The fielder ran as fast as he could, scooped up the ball in one graceful sweep, and threw a strike to the third baseman, putting-out the runner by ten feet. A roar went-up in the crowd and the young man turned back to us beaming.

He picked-up his hat, and as he started to trot into the infield to bat, he turned and asked, "What should I do now?" with a look of panic on his face. "I am the first batter this inning!"

Greg replied, "As my Uncle Jack always says, "Come on gang, let's rip!" So just grab a bat and let it rip!"

With that encouragement, we stayed just long enough to watch the young man hit a triple. With a big smile on his face, he turned from third base and gave us a 'thumbs-up' as we headed back to our car.

A few minutes later, we stopped at a country store for a pop and a bag of chips preparing for our trip home to Clinton County. In the window of the store, we could not help but notice a small sign that read: "For memory has painted this perfect day, with colors that never fade, and we find at the end of a perfect day, the soul of a friend we've made."

We looked at each other and smiled, uttering not a word. Words were not necessary. We understood how perfectly the message on the sign described our interaction with the young left fielder on that fateful day. Likely, we would never see him again; but no matter, that day was a very special day for us, indeed. And still is today.

The Men Who
Only Work on Sundays

A quick glance at the clock showed they had been working on unloading the refrigerator well more than 4 hours.

Yesterday was an anniversary of sorts. It marked the day our local big box store delivered our new refrigerator.

"When can you deliver it?" we asked.

"What about tomorrow?" the sales clerk asked. "We only deliver from 9 a.m. to 11 a.m. on Sundays." Reluctantly we agreed, hating to miss church, but with tight schedules it was our best option.

Sunday morning came and we had set about unloading the old refrigerator, placing all of the contents on ice. At approximately 9:00 a.m., we noticed the delivery truck parked down the street at a neighbor's house. Two hours later, we noticed the truck was still there. We found this a bit odd. Four hours passed. We decided they must have been having problems, which would probably result in them cancelling our delivery.

To our surprise, at about 4:45 p.m., the delivery truck appeared and began to back into our driveway. Friends had arrived for dinner and we were seated in the front room chatting.

One of the deliverymen, Russell, knocked at the front door and asked if this was the Haley residence. We confirmed that it was indeed. He apologized saying he and his partner, Ronnie, were late because they had run into some "unanticipated difficulties" at our neighbor's residence. Suddenly, it began to rain – and quickly turned unseasonably cold. Neither had worn a coat or a hat, just short sleeve shirts with the name of their store emblazoned across the front.

If you have ever seen the classic Laurel and Hardy movie, *The Music Box*, you would think you were about to see it reborn. In the movie, Stan and Ollie were a pair of bumbling movers, hired to move a piano up a ridiculously long flight of stairs to the home of an ill-tempered professor. One wrong-headed move after another keeps the piano tumbling back down the stairs, even after reaching the top. Unbeknownst to us, our delivery experience would turn out to be from the same page of misfortune.

The two men were amiable sorts, and worked tirelessly trying to get the refrigerator out of the box. After about twenty minutes, we walked into the garage and asked them how things were going. "We are having trouble getting this refrigerator out of the box," Russell said. We watched with fascination as the men continued to struggle. Finally, one cut the straps, tilted the box down, and pulled the refrigerator out of the box. We saw both men on the truck strapping the refrigerator to a "dolly."

They were now unable to make up their minds which one of them should stay on the truck and which one should work from ground level. I happily intervened and suggested the use of the automatic lift equipped on the truck. Sheepishly, the men agreed this was a good idea.

My friend looked-on with quiet amusement. Within minutes, they had lowered the refrigerator down onto the garage floor. Mistakenly, we felt the hard work was over. There was only one remaining step from the laundry room up into the long hallway that led into the kitchen. This time, we decided to stay and watch.

The men kept turning the dolly, first on its side then laying it flat. Then for some reason they determined they could not get the refrigerator into the hallway, so they decided to unstrap the refrigerator from the dolly and lift it into the house themselves. We silently questioned this maneuver but said nothing.

A quick glance at the clock showed they had been working on unloading the refrigerator well more than 4 hours.

After what seemed like an eternity, the men lowered the refrigerator and tried to carry the huge appliance, one at either end. Concerned for their safety, I suggested it would be easier if we placed rugs under the refrigerator to help slide it into place. They welcomed the offer and pondered another several minutes before deciding how best to place the rugs under the refrigerator.

We now knew why the men had arrived so late to deliver our order. After more time spent wrangling the piece and turning the corner from the hallway into the kitchen, the men stood the refrigerator upright. When they did, they misjudged the distance to the wall and suddenly we all heard a loud cracking sound. As my wife came to the kitchen, we both saw the large crack and dent on the side of our refrigerator. She immediately told the men she would not accept a damaged good saying, "You will have to return this refrigerator for a new one."

My friend and I quickly threw a bemused glance at each other. Both men were very apologetic and one said, "No problem." They said they would run back to the store, get a new refrigerator, and deliver a new item to us within 15 minutes.

Well, after almost 40 more minutes of maneuvering, the men finally had the scratched and dented refrigerator out of the kitchen. By this time, my friend and I were helping them as it was pouring a cold rain and both men were soaked to the bone.

They wheeled the cart to the edge of the truck. Finally, they would be on their way. As they were leaving, smiling and waving, they said they would get the new refrigerator and be right back. We were not optimistic to say the least. Finally, at approximately 11:00 p.m., we decided the men were not returning.

The next day, a young deliveryman arrived alone in the truck and said he was there to deliver our new refrigerator. We were skeptical. Within less than 8 minutes, the young man had the refrigerator unloaded, unstrapped, and assembled in placed in the kitchen. We asked what happened to the other two deliverymen.

"Oh, them. They only work on Sundays," he said with a smile.

Hoosiers: The Night David Beat Goliath

In fact, the game was such a victory for small towns, that in 1986 the movie 'Hoosiers' was born.

Basketball referees all across America will step to the middle of the court this week, blow their whistles, and toss the ball high in the air, as we tip-off another high school basketball tournament season.

Clinton County is no exception. The Blanchester Wildcats, the Clinton Massie Falcons, the East Clinton Astros, and the Wilmington Hurricane will begin tournament play in a variety of locations within the Miami Valley.

High school basketball tournaments are nothing new to Clinton County. A major difference is that during the 1950s and 1960s almost every village in Clinton County had a basketball team, and each team played in the county tournament at the old Fieldhouse in Xenia.

Some may be unaware that the teams of that era, including Adams, Blanchester, Clarksville, Jefferson, Martinsville, New Vienna, Port William, Reesville, Sabina, and Simon Kenton produced some of the best athletes ever to play within Clinton County.

Jack Haley, Don DeVoe, Donnie Fields, Butch Hooper, and Bobbie Hooper led the way for the Port William Bulldogs. Gary Rinehart was outstanding for the Rockets from Martinsville; and the Sabina Golden Eagles, coached by Buck Carter, led by sharp shooting guard Phil Snow, dominated the league for many years. Coach Tony Lamke often writes about these teams and their players in his delightful articles for the Wilmington News Journal.

The years passed, however, and government informed us it was necessary to consolidate our schools. The small village schools began to shut their doors, and the towns began to lose their identity. It was devastating because the schools were often the heart and soul of the community.

Our world is different today, but thankfully, some things never change. Clinton County fans will travel to the tournaments and root for the home team. Hope springs eternal with the hope that a David can still slay a Goliath.

A famous 'David versus Goliath' spirited basketball game took place on a snowy night in 1954 in Indianapolis, Indiana at the Butler Fieldhouse. Little Milan High School, located just 50 miles west of Cincinnati, played Muncie Central High School for the state championship.

Milan's entire school enrollment was little more than 150 students while Muncie Central had 1,662 students - a school ten times the size of Milan. Amazingly, Milan won the tournament at the buzzer with a last minute shot by Bobby Plump. This basketball game and its story has become an integral part of small-town basketball legend.

In fact, the game was such a victory for small towns, that in 1986 the movie *Hoosiers* was born, set in Knightstown, Indiana. Knightstown was similar to Milan like many rural towns we know. On the main street was located a bank, around the corner a post office, and at each end of town gas stations competed for the local business. In a sense, it is a place untouched by time.

One afternoon, my brother-in-law, Dick Butcher, and I were talking about the Hoosier movie and the Milan game. "I attended that game in Butler Fieldhouse, you know," Dick said. He said he and his teammates, along with his basketball coach, had driven up from Berne, Indiana to see the game expecting the powerhouse Muncie team to prevail. "The Fieldhouse was packed to the rafters, and the roar of the crowd was so loud you couldn't hear anything except the whistles of the referees," Dick continued. "When Bobby Plump made the final shot, complete pandemonium broke loose."

There was a particular scene in *Hoosiers* showing a string of vehicle taillights slowly winding through the rural Indiana countryside. Dick said he remembered seeing the taillights shining for miles as the cars slowly snaked their way homeward to Milan.

Last summer, my wife, Brenda, and I had the opportunity to stop in Knightstown to visit the "*Hoosier* Gym." The school was much like the ones we remember in the villages of Clinton County.

Neil Shaneyfelt, the caretaker, met us at the door. "Larry Bird was here a few years ago and shot baskets for an hour or so," Mr. Shaneyfelt said.

"Come with me," Mr. Shaneyfelt said. We followed him back up to the gym, and he handed us both a basketball. We, too, shot baskets for almost an hour.

"Folks, I am going to close in an about five minutes," Mr. Shaneyfelt said. As we prepared to leave, Brenda and I smiled at each other for we both knew what was going to happen next. I took the ball and carefully circled around the top of the key. I was in the exact spot where Bobby Plump took the final shot that had won the historic game. As Brenda counted down, "3, 2, 1," my feet left the floor for a jump shot that swished the net just as the imaginary buzzer rang.

For a moment, we both swore we could hear the crowd roar. However, it was only Mr. Shaneyfelt who said, "Take that moment home with you. You will be glad you did."

We replay this memory every year when it's time for the high school basketball tournaments to begin. We know that somewhere, in some small school, David will once again take on Goliath.

It is a story that bears repeating.

Hope is the Beacon that Brings Us Back

Like those POW's who placed their trust in the officers, we entrust our leaders to help rebuild our communities.

When my wife, Brenda, and I returned to Clinton County after living away several years, we saw many changes that excited us. People we knew, and some we've since met, were building homes. Subdivisions were growing, and equally as exciting, over one-hundred airplanes were flying into Wilmington every night. Yes, those changes excited us.

One night we set the alarm for 2:30 a.m. and rode out to the DHL Air Park. We watched as plane after plane landed and took-off in the misty morning air. The planes lit-up the runways and surrounding cornfields with their silvery blue lights. As they flew overhead, we marveled at the sheer excitement and activity, watching packages being unloaded, sorted, and flown to final destinations.

Business was thriving. Life was good. We couldn't have been happier that we'd returned home.

How could we have known? In less than a year, DHL would close and leave town.

Unemployment would soar to 21 percent. Home foreclosures would skyrocket. Some said a cloud of gloom had settled over the county ("Sagebrush would be blowing down Main Street," some whispered). Fear and sadness shook us, but in our hearts, we knew—jobs didn't make us who we are.

We needed to bounce back. We'd always found our way back from tough times.

In the process of tightening our belts, we've spent more time together. We've enjoyed more shows at the Murphy Theatre, shared time with friends at the General Denver, and listened to music at Friday night concerts sponsored by Downtown Wilmington. Village officials stepped forward, Wilmington College produced food, the Wilmington House of Prayer opened its doors, and My Father's Kitchen opened their hearts.

We had precedent, proof we could work together and meet any challenge. Four decades earlier, the former Clinton County Air Force Base, then a vital part of our county, had closed and left town. Tom Hunter, Don Babb, D. M. Fife, Maynard Davids, Bob Olinger, Jim Miller, and Bob Sollars of the Community Improvement Corporation (CIC) saw the threat in 1972. Strong leaders imbued with vision and a well-honed sense of local responsibility, they took action.

The CIC rolled-up their sleeves and went to work, transforming the abandoned Clinton County Air Force Base into an industrial park. Soon, several small businesses moved onto the Air Base. Ferno Washington was one of the first to arrive, and remains a treasure within our county today. Midwest Air Charter, Laurel

Oaks, Southern State, Kurz-Kasch, and Lift Trucks followed. Then, Airborne Freight arrived. Only eight years after the Air Force left, CIC burned the $1,200,000.00 mortgage. Success was returning to Clinton County.

Every generation has its leaders, those who emerge under pressure. Shortly after World War II ended, the British conducted a comparison study of the French, American, and British POW's held captive by the Germans. The researchers wanted to learn why the Americans had a higher rate of survival than did their counterparts, even though the Nazis used the same psychological techniques on all prisoners. Finally, an American Private-First Class who had been a prisoner for almost the entire war shed light on an interesting concept. He told the following story:

The Germans told the American, British, and French soldiers they would never live to see their loved ones again, walk the sidewalks of their hometowns, or celebrate Christmas. These tactics proved successful because many of the soldiers became depressed, dying in captivity.

One day, a German guard inside the prison walked past an American barracks, watching a group of soldiers surrounding an officer standing on a small table. The German soldier listened intently as the American officer told his men, "If you trust me, follow me, I will get you home safely." He was providing the soldiers hope, preventing them from becoming depressed and giving-up.

The German immediately informed his superiors what he had witnessed in the American barracks. The German high command ordered a team of German soldiers into the barracks, and without a word, they handcuffed the officer and removed him from the group.

Ironically, before they reached the end of the American barracks, the Germans turned around, hearing yet another American officer jump up, and rally his fellow POW's with these words: "If you trust me, follow me, I will get you home safely."

This same spirit lives today here in Clinton County. Many of the original CIC members are gone now. However, leaders of their generation passed on the torch to new leaders, who share the same vision and are willing to persevere to meet our present challenges.

Like those POW's who placed their trust in the officers, we entrust our leaders to help rebuild our communities. And it's working. We now see new construction. Fifth-Third Bank on Rombach is three months away from completion, and the Port Authority is building a new state-of-the-art hangar at the Air Park. A new airplane terminal is underway at Clinton Field. Several other businesses are also negotiating for the opportunity to locate in Clinton County.

It's a new day. Jobs are returning to our area. We are coming back, as we've a way of doing. We know it takes foresight, determination, and hard work.

But this isn't the first time it's ever been done.

Zimmie's –
The Last of a Kind

Climbing those narrow stairs to Zimmie's was a rite of passage, of sorts, at least in a young boy's mind.

I have found in telling this story it's difficult to separate reality from legend. The affection for the 'good old days', and the passage of time, has a way, of course, of coloring our memories.

Close your eyes and imagine a more bustling downtown Wilmington. We parked our car in a spot along the street. From there we walked to the post office and the bank. Then we would stop at Murphy-Benham Hardware to pick up some tools, or maybe Sheeter's Five and Ten to buy a pound of 'Nut Goodies' in bulk.

In those days, Wilmington was also home to a small, distinct restaurant with great food and unique ambience. For those too young to remember, it was nestled between Sheeter's Dime Store near the alley, and Ralph Fizer's bakery at the other end of North South Street. ·

Young boys eager to see what awaited them on the second floor at the top of the long, dark, wooden stairway, usually found what their fathers and grandfathers had found before them.

Two doors beckoned when you reached the

top of the stairs. The one on the left was long-rumored to contain illegal gambling, in the form of cards and billiards. The door on the right opened to the restaurant. Inside the smoke-filled walls, one found farmers, bankers, teachers, downtown merchants, and an assortment of others who simply had time on their hands, all eating some of the best steak sandwiches in town.

The name of the eatery was Zimmerman's Restaurant, commonly and affectionately referred to as simply 'Zimmie's.' Brothers Walter and Willard Zimmerman opened Zimmie's in 1920.

Zimmie's painted a lasting, vibrant portrait. There were pool tables in the back. Calendars and pictures of various topics adorned the walls. Some say even a spittoon was in the corner.

Over the years and still today, when asking friends if they had ever visited Zimmie's there is a common reaction. Eyes widen and light-up at once. You can see old memories tossing back and forth in their minds. Recently, one friend said with a small laugh, "Mom wouldn't allow me to go into the restroom alone when I was a small kid. She was afraid I might see some 'colorful' pictures."

As we reflect back over the years, we realize, in a way, climbing those narrow stairs to Zimmie's was a rite of passage, of sorts, at least in a young boy's mind. It represented passing from one's adolescence to young adulthood.

Maybe this is what draws some of us to these memories. Unlike the fast food restaurants of today that seem middling and throwaway, Zimmie's had whispered to us for decades - "Come to our sanctuary; a refuge from a reckless world. Zimmie's sat there perfectly content for 59 years, a place constant and secure."

On a summer day, feeling the breeze blowing, and smelling the gentle scent of rain after a brief shower, my uncle, Patsy Waldren, met my dad and me at Zimmie's for lunch. Although they severed beer, no one asked for ID's in those days. It was as if it was the most natural thing for an eight-year-old boy to be in an establishment that served liquor.

Nothing bad ever happened in Zimmie's. You could call it a beer joint, the kind you might see in an old movie, with a long bar and a large mirror on the back wall, but there never was a disturbance there.

It was a respectable, low-key establishment, affording its patrons the opportunity to escape for a few moments. As I grew older and entered high school, my ritual on Saturdays included lunch at Zimmie's. I always looked forward to the 'out-of-this-world' baked steak called the 'Hotshot,' French fries, and a 7-Up.

When our son, Greg, was six or seven years old, we continued the family tradition of eating lunch at Zimmie's. Greg soon started looking forward to our visits, and it wasn't long before he was hooked on the food. We even played a little pool, too.

Eventually, the Zimmerman brothers sold the restaurant to the Cole brothers, Dick and Bob. The Coles retained the name of Zimmie's for the restaurant. It maintained for over half a century its stanch upstairs reputation as a male-only bastion. Legend has it that even Bob Cole's daughter was not allowed to go upstairs. It was said she had to send a note up to her dad to come down to the sidewalk and meet her when needed.

Zimmie's, not exclusive in the sense of being fancy - exclusive in that it was a 'male-only' establishment. No one, not even the women, seemed to mind. It was merely a tradition, implying no prejudice. According to the old-timers, it was a time in society when an all-male exclusive club or restaurant could exist. I was just a boy at the time, so I didn't know or question those things.

As time went on, Bob and Dick Cole grew older themselves. They decided to sell the landmark business. Almost overnight, the old restaurant changed. Soon it was gone.

On August 17, 1979, Zimmie's closed. Downtown Wilmington lost a piece of its soul, and an era vanished.

Stopping a Runaway Truck

At that point, it was apparent the Fayette County officers would be hard-pressed to stop the racing vehicle.

It all began on a hot, quiet May afternoon day a little before 4:30 p.m. It was the kind of afternoon you might overhear a farmer talk about 'hearing the corn starting to grow' as the skies were clear and the wind was at rest. From a law enforcement perspective, the day had been uneventful.

I was Sheriff of Clinton County at the time, and was on patrol in the Sabina area. As I listened to the police radio, the Fayette County Sheriff's Office broadcasted that a semi-truck had caused a serious accident in the town of New Holland, Ohio, and had left the scene of the accident at a high rate of speed.

The dispatcher requested all Fayette County deputies be on the lookout for the fleeing vehicle. A short time later, another broadcast acknowledged the tractor-trailer rig was running cars off the roadway as he traveled toward the city of Washington Court House.

We soon heard as the Court House Police Department dispatcher said the wayward truck had entered their city limits. The truck had struck two vehicles as it roared through red lights, causing considerable damage.

The Fayette County dispatcher then described the truck as speeding through town and having struck several more vehicles. Suddenly, and with resounding urgency in his voice, a Washington Court House police officer stated he was directly behind the speeding truck. However, he said the truck driver failed to stop and, in fact, was accelerating at an alarming rate of speed.

At that point, it was apparent the Fayette County officers would be hard-pressed to stop the racing vehicle. I contacted the Clinton County Sheriff's Dispatch Center and instructed them to advise all available deputies to drive toward US Routes 22 and 3, just east of Wilmington. The radio traffic continued, with Fayette County officers frantically describing how the truck was weaving back and forth in the roadway forcing oncoming traffic into the ditch.

As a group of Clinton County deputies awaited on alert, suddenly, we caught glimpse of a long line of cruisers approaching with their lights flashing, following behind the truck. To our surprise, no one was initiating the lead to stop the wayward vehicle. We learned the Officer-In-Charge of Washington, C.H. had instructed his officers simply to follow behind the truck. They were not to attempt to stop it.

This placed added pressure on our department. At speeds approaching 100 miles-per-hour, the semi-truck was like a missile heading directly toward the highly populated areas of Clinton County.

The immediate question at hand was whether to take action

and stop the truck at the risk of injuring others, or allow the out-of-control tractor-trailer to enter the corporation limits of Wilmington? It was a difficult decision. We acted. The officers set up two roadblocks: the first on US 22 and 3, in order to stop the eastbound flow of traffic toward the truck; and the second, closer to the oncoming truck, near Melvin, on the same highway. It was our hope the truck would pull over upon seeing the roadblock.

The roadblock just outside of Wilmington was successful, with traffic coming to a complete stop. However, the second roadblock was not. The fleeing truck blew through the Melvin roadblock with approximately thirteen police cruisers in active pursuit.

Our fleet of deputies were in position. As the wayward truck passed through Melvin toward Wilmington, we signaled Lieutenant Randy Cline to shoot the tires of the truck to disable the vehicle.

Suddenly, we heard a loud roar coming toward us, and immediately we saw the truck heading toward Stone Road at a speed of approximately 85 miles per hour. We asked the Fayette County authorities to fall back.

Lieutenant Cline then performed one of the most remarkable feats that I witnessed throughout my law enforcement career. As the truck fast approached Starbuck Road, two shots bellowed from Lieutenant Cline's shotgun. Incredibility, both shots hit the tires squarely on target. The truck slowly came to a stop exactly at the intersection of Route 22 and Starbuck Road.

I have looked back many times with amazement at Lieutenant

Cline's ability to place two shotgun slugs, in rapid succession, into a vehicle tire with the vehicle traveling at such a high rate of speed. Many can adjust to situations that are predictable; however, very few can adapt to high-stress conditions with such accuracy. It is remarkable to think Lieutenant Cline's life-saving actions occurred in the midst of pumping adrenaline and overwhelming excitement. No doubt, the Lieutenant's ability to remain calm and focused in the midst of crisis was a major part in determining the success or failure of the mission.

Lieutenant Cline's actions very likely saved innocent lives.

Lieutenant Randy Cline passed away on Monday, October 10, 2011. He was a good man and a fine officer, indeed.

Cherokee Bill, an man of the Old West with a Mighty Steady Hand

Cherokee Bill didn't merely tack a bull's eye on a board. His marksmanship brought you to the edge of your seat.

The Haley family moved to North Spring Street in the summer of 1963. It was a quiet, pleasant street, tree-lined and stretching from Locust Street to Xenia Avenue. One of the most charming neighborhoods in Wilmington.

A boyhood friend, Roger Vaughan, lived across the alley on Mulberry Street. We spent many summer evenings throwing baseballs to each other in the middle of the street, pausing just long enough to allow an occasional car to pass-by.

My brother, Jack, and his family lived next door. In fact, he and Nancy still live in the same house today. My sister, Rita, and her family have lived at the other end of North Spring Street in the same house since September, 1965.

We have seen many friends and neighbors come and go over the years. Jerry Burton, Bill Fife, Bill and Mark 'Tutt' Taylor and their family, and Carol Jones DeFayette just to name a few. Haywood's Market was located in the middle of the block, as many neighborhood markets were back then.

Walking up or down North Spring Street in those days, we often saw our good neighbors, Mr. and Mrs. Harley Day; Dwight and Marjorie Drummond; Bob and Frankie Baker; Gene and Sharon Breckel; Farrell and Carole Nichols; Kenny and Jan Vaughn; Harold and Helen Gehringer; Barb and Terry Urton; Dorothy Walker; Paul and Jean Riley, and many others, working in their yards or sitting on the porch.

Then, one day, a man rode into town in an old Cadillac. The car had large bullhorns mounted to the car's grill, with huge twin fender horns on each side. These were not bullhorns used for voice amplification, but real bullhorns - ones that at one time had sat on the head of a long-horned bull somewhere in Texas or Oklahoma!

The man was dressed in a brown cowboy hat, western shirt with an ascot tie, brown and white cowboy boots, and western pants that would have made Roy Rogers blush. Strapped around his trim waist were twin Colt .45 revolvers.

His name was Cherokee Bill. He moved in two doors down from my sister, Rita.

Cherokee Bill was a Native American born in 1901 on an Indian Reservation in Oklahoma. He left the reservation at about nine years of age to travel with the Wild Bill Wild West Show. His job was to throw potatoes in the air while riding a horse backwards, as another trick-shooter rode behind on another horse, shooting the objects in mid-air.

After a few years, he started his own Chief Cherokee Bill Show. An expert sharpshooter, he traveled the country entertaining school kids, county fairs goers, and anyone that gathered in small towns to watch them perform.

Cherokee Bill didn't merely tack a paper bull's eye on a board. His marksmanship brought you to the edge of your seat. As a volunteer from the audience would throw a nickel twenty feet in the air, everyone gasped as Cherokee Bill put a hole in it before it hit the ground. Bill could shoot, throw knives, ride horses, and even snap a cigarette from a volunteer's mouth with his bullwhip ten-feet away.

In his shows, Cherokee Bill would ask an audience member to step to the stage as he bent at the waist, cracking his whip just above their head. The whip would gently wrap around their necks ever so slightly, like a water snake catching minnows.

A man from a bygone era, Cherokee Bill played spoons on schoolchildren's' heads, balanced a ladder or chair on his chin, and threw knives shearing off the tips of cigarettes from the mouths of nervous volunteers. He even shot cigarettes in half as the glowing butt dangled from their shaking lips.

One summer evening, my sister Rita remembers Cherokee Bill announcing that he would be performing a portion of his show for the North Spring Street neighbors. He asked one of the neighbors, Mary, to be his partner for the special neighborhood show.

Rita said the neighbors were antsy. At that time in his career, it was rumored Cherokee Bill's eyesight was beginning to fail. As good neighbors do, however, they diligently tromped over to his side yard and waited for the show to begin. Mary stood calmly with a cigarette in her mouth and her eyes closed, as Cherokee aimed his pistol at her. To the delight of the adults and children alike, he shot off the end of the smoking cigarette right before their eyes.

Then, Cherokee Bill threw a dime into the air and shot at it. He then picked-up the dime, which had a hole in it.

"The most amazing trick was about to happen as the crowd began to grow," Rita said as her hands began to sweat. Mary was calm as she jumped in front of a large board as Cherokee Bill began to throw knives around her. Before long, Mary's body began to shake like Don Knotts as each knife commenced to outline her torso. With each additional throw, the neighbors began to groan. As he threw the last knife Cherokee Bill yelled, "Oh, no!" The knife headed directly toward Mary's midsection. Suddenly, Cherokee Bill began to laugh. He showed the crowd the knife he had just thrown at Mary was a rubber knife.

Every once in a great while, you run across a man who you never forget. Cherokee Bill was such a person.

Cherokee Bill Verne, a very nice man, died on April 25, 1978 from heart failure and pneumonia.

The Man from the Mountains Played Bluegrass in Gettysburg

We could sense they were worried he would disrupt their music.

If you've ever ventured across the mountains to Gettysburg, Pennsylvania, you no doubt may have visited the small, unique music store just down from the James Getty Hotel on Chambersburg Street. Years ago, Brenda and I came across the Arrow Horse Music Store one evening while strolling along the borough's town square.

The Arrow Horse is beyond description, in a way. The store houses an unusual combination of antiques and musical instruments, while serving as an oasis for those who follow the bluegrass sound.

When we first walked through the doors of the Arrow Horse, we noticed the large, wooden plank floor, much like those seen in downtown businesses in the 1950s. There is little decor - just a mixture of assorted wooden stools and plastic chairs for visitors to use, and a variety of banjos, guitars and fiddles for sale hanging from the ceiling. The Arrow Horse feels like an old time country store, a place where the mountain people of the Appalachians gathered years ago to share music.

Larry Noel is probably the best musician of the group. On one of our first visits, we heard one of the other musicians call him 'Ike'. I once approached him and made a request," Ike, do you know the song, My Old Love Letters?" Although he looked at me funny, I just thought he wasn't used to getting requests from the audience. It was nearly two years later before we learned his name was Larry. President Dwight 'Ike' Eisenhower made Gettysburg his home for many years, and obviously the nickname was a bit of whimsy on the part of the musicians.

Gettysburg is, of course, a tourist town with a steady ebb and flow of visitors each week. This year marks the 150th Anniversary of the battle. One evening while sitting in the Arrow Horse, several Civil War re-enactors in full Confederate military regalia entered the store. One of the musicians, a mandolin player named Johnny Brown, yelled out, "Are we under attack again?" No one missed a beat.

The group of musicians and the regular audience members have become like family over time. Their special relationship became evident when the front door opened one evening and in walked a man taller than most with a fair complexion, almost pale, and the sharp, proud lean features of a man who had spent time in mountains. He was carrying a battered, worn guitar case.

He was younger than most of the musicians, near fifty or so, and walked with a high degree of difficulty. He was trembling. His speech was uncertain and quivering. At first, he sat in the audience and listened to the music. Within a short while he began to take his guitar out of its case. We noticed several of the musicians glance at each other. We could sense they were worried he would disrupt their music.

After much effort, the man removed the guitar, strapped it around his shoulder and started for the empty stool in the middle of the circle of musicians. It was difficult for him. He laughed nervously as he climbed halfway up the stool and plunked down.

"Would you like to sing a song?" one of the musicians asked. The banjo picker gave his fellow musician a dirty look. He felt the man was unnecessarily being cruel.

"Yes, I would. I'd like to sing a song," the man said - his voice a little stronger, as we noticed the stranger's hands had stopped trembling. "This is the first time in two years I've been out of my house. I love music, but haven't played since my sweet wife of twenty-seven years died two springs ago," the man said to the now hushed room.

All of the eyes in the room were on this most unlikely man as he played the first clear notes on his guitar and began to sing in a beautiful lyrical tenor voice a haunting love song.

There was stunned amazement as the man quietly finished playing the song, awkwardly climbed down from the stool, and walked halfway back to his chair.

"You did a wonderful job on that song," I told him.

"Grab hold of those you love, and hang on to'em real tight," he whispered slowly in his soft Appalachian manner as he put away his guitar and closed the case, "When my wife was sick, I died a little bit every day along with her. Our love was a gift and on loan to us, and it lasts only for a blink of an eye."

"Yes. I know," I replied quietly. "I know."

The chance meeting and the gentleman's words spoke powerfully to me back then and carries through still today, reminding me of how precious my wife, my family and many friends are to me.

We heard just recently that the Arrow Horse is gone now, too. Sometimes we never appreciate enough until we realize something is over in our life.

The Summer Davy Crockett visited Port William

We all treasure innocence, wishing we could put those memories in a bottle and tuck them away forever.

Our grandson, Jack, is an innocent, happy young boy. Letters on his bedroom wall spell-out the words laugh, learn, and love.

When he was three-years old, Jack and I walked down the street together hand-in-hand.

Suddenly, Jack came to a complete stop. He began waving at two of his young friends as they were leaving home with their parents. "Can you come over, Jack?" the boy shouted.

"Bye, Audrey. Bye, Tyler," Jack said tenderly, as he waved to the little girl and boy.

I quietly marveled at the innocence and heartfelt love in Jack's tender, warm voice as he bid his friends good-bye. Jack was thrilled to see his friends, but sad to see them leaving their shared world of rocks, puppies, and leaf piles.

"Jack, that was very nice of you to say good-bye to your friends," I said as we waved to the passing car as we journeyed down the street.

Like his dad, Greg, Jack seizes the little things, the important things in life. A couple of months ago, Brenda and I watched as Jack excitedly played basketball with his team. Jack doesn't just run, he bounces and skips all over the floor. He will occasionally touch the ball, but rarely shoots or dribbles. On the way home from the game, I heard Jack ask his dad, "Dad, did you see me smile at you every time I got the ball?"

"I sure did," Greg replied. Jack loves putting a basketball through a hoop, but he loves his dad more and he wanted his dad to know it.

We all treasure innocence, wishing we could put those memories in a bottle and tuck them away forever. In a sense we do. Those of us who grew up in the 1950s and the 1960s knew innocent times. We knew that Roy Rogers was King of the Cowboys and Dale Evans was, of course, Queen of the West.

In fact, cowboy heroes Roy Rogers, Hopalong Cassidy, and the Lone Ranger all had Codes of Conduct that spelled-out the rules. Those simple rules transcend time. I find them still applicable in life today.

The Lone Ranger Code of Conduct said, I believe:
- *That to have a friend, a man must be one.*
- *Everyone has within himself the power to make this a better world.*
- *That man should live by the rule of what is best for the greatest number.*
- *In my Creator, my country, my fellow man.*

As young boys, we believed in that code. Much of the summer was occupied, as one might guess, playing 'Cowboys and Indians.'

One of our favorite places to play was just beyond the Maple Grove Cemetery. There was a mysterious mound resting in the middle of the cemetery. Some told us it was an old Indian burial mound, full of ancient artifacts. A more pragmatic friend said it was just a pile of rocks covered with grass. We never knew for sure and we didn't care, but we liked to think the mound was remnant of a time when wild Indians roamed the wilds of Port William. That theory was okay with a boy whose hero was Davy Crockett.

Many years later, when my son, Greg, was a young boy, we drove to Port William. I proudly showed him my old playground. I told him when I was his age, about eight or nine, I loved playing 'Cowboys and Indians' near the cemetery. I pointed-out the grapevines and showed him the stream I had followed to Paintersville Road. Greg loved the story. Especially when I told him Grandpa Haley once walked with me as we followed the stream all the way across town.

A year or so ago, Greg and I returned to Port with Grandson Jack in tow. Taking the same trip, I happily told Jack the familiar story. As a boy who loves police officers, firefighters and Navy Seals, Jack found the stories about his grandpa pretending to fight the wild Indians in Port William fascinating. "It was right over there where our horses used to stand," I told Jack as we both smiled as we pictured the imaginary corral. "I would sneak over to the edge of the field and watch the Indians dance around a large campfire," I told Greg and Jack. "Sometimes they would even chase me home," I added with an easy grin.

A few weeks ago, Greg and Jack came for another visit. Our travels included another trip to Port William. When we turned on Paintersville Road, Jack who is seven-years-old, turned to me and said, "Grandpa, you did a good job."

I looked at him and said, "What do you mean, Jack?"

He said again, "You did a good job."

Greg erased the puzzled look on my face when he said, "Jack believes you did a good job. There are no wild Indians in Port William."

We all laughed. The most important thing in Jack's world at that instant was my story about playing 'Cowboy and Indians', which in turn, made that particular moment the most important in mine. As we put our memories back in the bottle for the day, we knew that although some things pass away the innocence we pass from generation to generation lasts forever. The little things may turn out to be the most important things after all.

Gunfire on South Street

I know there is no sound like a gun fired in anger. Especially in downtown Wilmington. In the middle of the night.

"Get out of the car with your hands in the air." Those are words most of us hear only in the movies. Those words were spoken in real life on September 23, 1970, on North South Street, at 2:15 a.m. in the morning.

It's been forty-two years ago this week since that fateful day. As a new police officer with the Wilmington Police Department, I and another officer were involved in a shootout with three escaped prisoners.

Having joined the Wilmington Police Department just three months prior in June 1970, and at the age of 22, I had no prior police training. I had never shot a revolver—that is, with the exception of a .22 caliber pistol.

It was a quiet night. There was little radio traffic. The cruising of the city had been uneventful. Up to that point. Suddenly, just as I turned the police cruiser off Curtis Drive onto Lincoln Street, the police dispatcher, David Lieurance, gave a general broadcast to "be on the lookout for a 1956 Ford, black with a red hood."

The car contained three escapees from the Lawrence County jail. Witnesses had seen the car earlier in the Portsmouth, Ohio area, where the escapees had briefly taken an Ohio State Highway Trooper hostage. One of the escapees was wanted for armed robbery. Another for burglary. And the third for auto larceny.

Within minutes after the broadcast, I heard Officer Bob Stratton advise he was behind the suspect vehicle, and was preparing to stop it at the location of North South Street and Xenia Avenue. I could hardly believe my ears.

As I turned south onto South Street, I immediately saw Officer Stratton's cruiser near the Xenia Avenue intersection with its lights flashing. I drove directly past the escapees' vehicle, and I could clearly see the three fugitives sitting inside.

Just as I opened my cruiser door, I observed Stratton approach the escapees' car. I was only about ten yards away. Suddenly, I heard yelling, a single gunshot, and then bang, bang, bang, bang. Four gunshots in rapid succession. Officer Stratton retreated back toward his cruiser, firing his revolver as he ran.

At that point, I was standing alone in the middle of Lorish Avenue just behind the two police cruisers, groping for my revolver. I pointed my gun at the suspects for what seemed like hours, although I know it was only for a few minutes.

Then, there was no more gunfire. Quietly, I called to Officer Stratton. I asked if he was okay. Fortunately, he replied that he was unharmed. In turn, I told him I was all right, too. Then there was stillness.

All at once the late Sergeant Charlie Lyons roared onto the

scene. Sergeant Lyons grabbed his shotgun and ran toward the fugitives' car. "Get out of the car with your hands in the air," I heard him shout. At that point, we all looked beyond the car to see a man, Guy Wolfe, Jr., lying in the street mortally wounded. We removed the two remaining escapees, Joe Sanders and Larry Clay, from the car and placed them under arrest.

After the shooting, I drove to my home on Spring Street in Wilmington. I woke up my mom to tell her about the incident. Surprisingly, she remained calm. In a gentle voice, she said, "I don't know why such a nice, easy going young man like you wants to be in police work."

At that particular time, I was no longer sure myself.

Many years have gone by since that night. And since then, I have spent many hours at firing ranges and hearing the sounds of guns. But as I look back, I know there is no sound like a gun fired in anger. Especially, in downtown Wilmington. In the middle of the night.

There's never a time when I drive by that I don't glance over at that spot on North South Street. Today the mailbox is gone and so are many of the families that lived there. But one night back in the seventies, there was an old black and red Ford. And three escapees. And when the stillness, darkness, and shadows all come together at the right moment, I can still see the pain of living and the fear of death, every time I look that way.

The Young Girl on Seventy-Two

A small, blue car was smoking and against a tree, with several feet of fence wrapped around it.

The warm May evening was slowly melting into the clear darkness of night as I headed home to Sabina from a busy day at the Sheriff's Office. It would be good to be home.

The radio in the cruiser had been unusually quiet for the last hour or so, and maybe the frantic activity of the day was over. Just as I entered the crossroads town of Reesville, the radio dispatcher broke the quiet with an urgent message:

"There is a report of a Code 4, with serious injury, on State Route 72, about two miles south of 22 and 3 East. The Ohio State Highway Patrol and the life squad are enroute," the radio crackled with urgency.

I covered the last couple of miles quickly, arriving at the scene of the accident within sixty seconds of the radio broadcast. A small, blue car was smoking and leaning against a tree, with several feet of fence wrapped around it. One wheel was still spinning. An elderly farmer was leaning into the car, quietly brushing the windshield glass away from the eyes of a young girl, lying injured on the front seat. I could see the relief in the farmer's face when he saw my uniform.

The teenager looked to be about sixteen or seventeen years of age. It was apparent she had sustained a serious head injury. Lowering myself into the front seat of the car, the farmer pulled himself clear and gladly changed places with me, but remaining nearby. I moved across the seat and gently placed the head of the young girl on a towel. As I began talking to her, I soon found myself asking the hopeful question I had often heard asked at the scene of many accidents: "Are you okay?" She didn't answer. The ashen color in her face told me she was in very serious condition. With one hand, I carefully wiped the shreds of glass from her face. As I gazed down upon the young girl, I could see the deep brown eyes that were the centerpiece of her pretty face.

The two sounds occurred almost simultaneously; the slow, lazy, moan of a siren in the distance, and a soft, gentle murmur from the girl. She had scarcely uttered the sounds, when I saw she was beginning to slip away. She opened her eyes and I felt a ray of hope. I want to think perhaps in those precious moments of her life, my face might have become a composite of her mother, her dad, and maybe a younger brother still at home.

I spoke to her in a gentle, caring tone and quietly reassured her. We both knew it was too late.

A few seconds after intoning those words, the young girl who had just celebrated her last day of school for the year, began to lose consciousness. Her labored breathing began to lower the veil between life and death.

She directed one last gaze at me. With time so short, there was nothing more that could be done other than to make her comfortable.

The young girl gently closed her eyes and our focus shifted from her earthly body to her spirit.

I could hear the farmer gently crying above me as I carefully lowered the young girl's head down onto the seat of the car. The sirens we had heard in the distance had arrived too late. The farmer and I gazed quietly at one another for a moment, each with a heavy heart and moistened eyes. Slowly, I began to walk back to the cruiser.

My mind slowly shifted to the impending duty most-dreaded by law enforcement; the delivery of a death notice to the family. How does one tell someone his or her loved one was never coming home again?

Several years before, I had arrived at a farmhouse to deliver a death notice at about 6:30 in the morning. At that time, the victim was a family's seventeen-year-old son. "Why don't you go in?" another deputy asked me.

"I want them to have one more hour of peaceful sleep," I told the deputy. "It may be the last peaceful night's sleep they have for the rest of their lives."

Spring is a time of rebirth and renewal. I share these sad experiences for I know this is also the approaching time for high school proms. Throughout April and May, young men in rented tuxedoes appear along with beautiful young girls dressed in gowns with flowers. My wish for each of them is to have fun. My prayer for each of them is to be safe. It is a time for making wonderful lifelong memories.

Please don't end-up like the young man, or the young woman on Seventy-Two.

Remembering the Xenia Tornado

We stood silently, listening to the commotion. The motorcade was heading directly toward our family as we stood outside Tecumseh Elementary School in Xenia, Ohio. A horrific tornado had just destroyed our home a few days before.

The President of the United States had come to Xenia, raising the spirits of the people with words of comfort, reassurance, and promise. As soon as the President stuck his head out of his car, a cheer went up. He stepped out of the long, black limousine. He looked sad.

It just so happened I was the first person he saw. He came over, shook my hand, and put his arm around my shoulder.

"It's the worst disaster I've ever seen," President Richard Nixon said kindly. "We are here to help, and you will be fine."

"Thank you, Mr. President. We appreciate your kindness," I responded.

Today marks an anniversary of shared memories of loss and rebuilding. We remember the unified efforts of those who stood together helping the wounded, sustaining the homeless, reconstructing the homes, schools, and community, in what was and still is today the most terrible ten minutes in the history of Xenia, Ohio.

Most of us remember where we were and what we were doing on that fateful day of April 3, 1974. I was working in Dayton, Ohio and had just finished talking on the telephone with my mother. She had invited our family to have dinner with her and my father that evening.

"Why don't you take off an hour early to beat the heavy Dayton traffic?" my boss suggested. I gladly accepted his thoughtful invitation. Shortly after arriving home, we loaded the car and headed south on U.S. 68 enroute to my parent's home on Spring Street in Wilmington. I had glanced at the clock on the way out of the house, and noted it was about 3:35 p.m. The day had been beautiful and sunny, but as I walked down the driveway, I noticed the clouds had become full and puffy, typical of an early spring day in the Miami Valley. There was nothing in the atmosphere at that time to make us suspicious, although I remember looking in the rear view mirror a few times thinking to myself how the sky had taken on a gloomy look with just a hint of green mixed within the various low-hanging clouds.

Mom and Dad greeted us at the door and invited us in for dinner. Mom had the food prepared, and we immediately sat down at the large wooden table in the dining room. The meal began on an upbeat note as Grandpa Haley teased our son, Greg. Suddenly, a news flash from a local TV station interrupted the jovial banter. The National Weather Service had issued a warning that a large, powerful tornado had just touched down at 4:40 p.m. in the Arrowhead Subdivision in Xenia – the subdivision where our home was situated - our home that we had left just an hour earlier.

My first thought was that the tornado was probably a minor storm that had caused some barns to lose a few roofs, or at worst, uprooted a few trees. My opinion quickly changed when we called one of our neighbors who said, "Your home no longer exists." The neighbor continued, "Your house is gone. My husband just returned from there looking through all of your rubble and trying to find your wife and son. He couldn't find them. We are so sorry." I reassured her they were safe with me, but her news stunned me.

The following morning, when we turned onto Commonwealth Drive, our street, my mind nearly shut down in total disbelief. The area looked like a war zone. There were helicopters flying overhead, National Guard troops were patrolling the streets, and Red Cross vans were scurrying from driveway to driveway looking for additional victims.

Although the area was inherently familiar to us having lived there for almost two years, we quickly became disoriented. We found ourselves unable to identify once familiar streets – debris hanging from the overhead power and telephone lines. Homes built on slabs with no basements were now only slabs of concrete. Our neighbors passed by in the streets crying, some after finding the body of a loved one.

I still ponder the gravity of it all. I cannot imagine what it must have been like for those who lost family members to realize their loved ones were gone forever. Was there a final glance at one another, or maybe a final word? It is too difficult to comprehend such pain. I know had our plans been altered that day, our family might quite possibly have found ourselves in that very situation.

Rich Heiland, a former classmate from high school, worked for the Xenia Gazette at the time of the tornado. Rich said it best: "We should all be dead today, as, sadly, too many are. But we are alive, and we will be back, and we will survive."

We had survived, thankfully. We learned life is fragile. None of us knows the length of our days.

The Man
from Lonesome Town

102 — The Storyteller: Growing Up in Clinton County, Ohio

When Ricky first came into his dressing room at the Murphy, he was very shy.

A few weeks ago, my friend, Danny Mongold, and I were talking about the concerts that he, Jerry Bryant, Jim Smith, and Harold Chrisman, sponsored at the Murphy Theatre in the 1980's.

We remembered how the Murphy sold out when Marty Robbins, Bill Anderson, Ernest Tubb, and Loretta Lynn performed. The place overflowed, however, when Rick Nelson was live in concert.

My brother, Jack, who was a Wilmington City Police officer at the time, and I as the county sheriff, had the pleasure of providing security for the musical artists who performed during those years. Being the only two officers on duty, Jack and I spent most of our time near the performers' dressing room to keep overzealous fans away from the stars. We had the opportunities to make small talk with most of the performers, many that were at the zenith of their careers.

Marty Robbins was popular with the local

crowds, although one became the victim of his wrath. A fan from Wilmington asked him if he was going to stop at the local bus station on Sugartree Street for a late night snack. "No, we have to be in Buffalo, New York tomorrow night," Marty responded.

"Bill Anderson did," the lady said pressing her luck.

"Well, then you will just have to call Bill Anderson. He's in Nashville," Marty said as he walked back to his bus.

The one performer who particularly sticks out in my mind is Ricky Nelson. His appearance was striking. His hair was thick and wavy brown, worn long over the sides. His eyes were the bluest I'd ever seen.

In the middle of his career, Ricky had changed his named to "Rick." Danny Mongold told me how he made the mistake of calling him Ricky, and soon found out the performer could be very direct with his language. "My name is Rick Nelson, not Ricky Nelson," he said.

Interestingly, a few years later Carl Perkins, the Rockabilly singer, had this to say about Rick Nelson: "I only know two cats in this business that really had it all; Elvis was one of those guys, the other was Ricky Nelson. There was a difference in those guys though. Elvis moved. Ricky never had to. He stood flat-footed and captivated his audience with his good looks. We grew up with him; those who didn't missed something. History books are gonna have to say that he played a big role in Rock 'n' Roll music. And he did it his way."

Carl later met Rick in Memphis one day and said to him, "Ricky, there's only a couple of us originals left." Out of respect to

Carl, he went back to calling himself "Ricky" again.

When Ricky first came into his dressing room at the Murphy, he was very shy. He spoke a barely audible "hi" to Jack and me. He was self-conscious but extremely polite. We briefly exchanged small talk and asked if he had a good flight in from California. He said he did, and thanked us for our assistance. He asked us how we liked police work, and said that he had always wanted to be a police officer. This man known all over the world for three decades, seemed to enjoy talking with us about Wilmington. He appeared almost wistful and said several times that those who lived in small towns might hold the secret to life. He said that he always wanted to live in a small town and raise a family (one like Ozzie and Harriet I thought to myself?).

I am not impressed easily, but I instantly liked and admired this humble man. Jack and I had an opportunity to stand just outside the dressing room listening to Ricky and his guitarist practice for a few minutes before the show. I first heard the familiar strains of "They'll Never Be Any One Else but You" sung with that familiar voice. He sang a few bars to warm-up. The guitarist played a tenor guitar and practiced a song well-known to me, "Lonesome Town". Rick joined in and they practiced their vocal harmony in front of us. It was a magical, almost dreamlike moment. As Paul McCartney said, "I liked Rick Nelson. I love 'Lonesome Town'. It's a place we all know."

December 31, 2012, marked twenty-seven years ago, since I was stunned to learn, along with millions of other people in the world, that Ricky Nelson had crashed into a cornfield, perished and died.

George Jones and the Night
Webb Pierce Sang Off-Key

No other performers in show business dressed or looked like the old Grand Ole Opry starts.

"George Jones, a master of sad country ballads whose voice held the bracing power, the sweetness, and the burn of an evening's final pull from a bourbon bottle, died last Friday morning at a Nashville hospital. Often called the greatest male vocalist in country music history, the 'King of Broken Hearts' just broke many more," according to the Nashville Tennessean.

Death and funerals are nothing new to country music. The 2003 interment of Johnny Cash, a good friend of "the Possum", became somewhat of a state funeral in Nashville. Thousands of mourners lined lower Broadway, as customers peeked out of Tootsie's Lounge and the Ernest Tubb Record Shop hoping for one last glimpse of Johnny. All flags flew at half-mast.

However, there's always a story behind the sequins. A friend of mine, a man we shall call Chas, owned a celebrity protection business. One of his clients was another well-known country singer. According to Chas, the singer had received a serious death threat from a stalker a few months earlier, and ever since that time, had retained Chas as his personal bodyguard.

The singer called Chas and told him he wanted to attend Johnny Cash's funeral, and he wanted Chas to accompany him. On the day of the funeral, Chas drove to the church to scope-out the detail. When he arrived, he saw approximately two-hundred limousines lined-up and ready to proceed to the cemetery. Chas introduced himself to the funeral director and told him he needed to get to the cemetery early in order to secure the area prior to his client's arrival. "Where would you like to position me within the procession," Chas inquired.

"Why don't you pull-in right behind the three motorcycle officers? That will give you ample time to secure the premises," the other 'Man in Black' said.

Later, as the bells tolled twelve o'clock noon, the black cars rolled-out. With his famous boss in tow, Chas followed behind the motorcycle police as the procession began its' journey toward Johnny's final resting place. All the while, Chas allowed his mind to wander as they snaked their way to the cemetery. Suddenly, Chas redirected his attention as the three motorcycle officers roared-off streaking down the line to block several intersections.

Then it dawned on Chas. He was now leading the funeral procession toward Hendersonville, with a famous singer in the back seat, and he didn't have a clue as to the location of the cemetery! Further, he was on live television. Slightly in a panic, yet slightly amused, Chas said he did the only thing he could think of doing at the time - he called me and said - "Guess where I'm at, and guess what I'm doing?" It was a surreal moment.

After a few minutes of quiet alarm, Chas said he unexpectedly spotted another 'Man in Black' standing in the street, motioning the solemn mourners inside the cemetery. Relieved, to say the least, Chas pulled into the drive with the full funeral procession behind him, as if he knew exactly what he was doing and where he was going. With that, Chas leaned back in his seat, let out a roar of laughter, and said with a broad smile, "Nashville is a fun town!"

Nashville has been like no other place in the world. No other performers in show business dressed or looked like the old Grand Ole Opry stars; and definitely, no one else talked or acted like them. Where else could you hear a performer say he had been plowing a field with a mule all afternoon before he came to the Opry House? It had been decades since farmers last used mules to plow ground. No matter, if you were an Opry star you still rode a mule and either picked cotton or 'ate tators for supper'.

Many years ago, I attended the Grand Ole Opry as part of the entertainment arranged by the National Sheriffs' Association. The number of stars performing on that particular night was amazing. At a time when country music was still country, Johnny Cash, George Jones, Dolly Parton, Hank Snow, Loretta Lynn, and many other stars entertained the enthusiastic crowd.

Suddenly, a performer bounded onto stage wearing a pale blue Nudie suit bedecked with hundreds of sparkling rhinestones, carrying a guitar around his neck. The singer, Webb Pierce, was a pioneer singer in country music history beginning his career in the 1950's. Webb strummed a few chords and began to sing, "There Stands the Glass" when a strange thing began to happen. A woman sitting in front of me leaned over to her husband and asked, "Who is that guy?"

"That's Webb Pierce; the old country singer," I heard him whisper. "He has a guitar-shaped swimming pool in his backyard."

The woman then commented that Webb was singing extremely off-key. The more Webb sang, the angrier the woman became. Ironically, she began to take her anger out on her husband--- just because he had heard of Webb Pierce, I guess. She wouldn't let-up, becoming more and more upset because he was singing terribly off-key. When he started to sing "In the Jailhouse Now," the woman was livid.

"Well, don't get mad at me. I didn't invite him to sing," the husband finally turned and told his wife with a puzzled look on his face.

Johnny Cash and Webb Pierce, as well as, George Jones, are all gone now. Although a little piece of history has died with each of them, somehow we move on and never look back. But, oh, what great memories.

Moon River

A lazy stream of dreams, where vain desires forget themselves in the loveliness of sleep.

During the depths of the Great Depression, Powel Crosley, Jr., owner of WLW Radio, called his people at his radio station. He told them to come up with a new sign-off program that would be soothing and relaxing. "None of that dance music," he ended, "and I want it ready for airing tomorrow night."

The original Moon River program included a violin, a female trio, a narrator, and a theatre organ. As a young boy, I can remember listening to the program each night before I drifted off to sleep. The program came on at about 11:00 p.m. and lasted until midnight. It was popular throughout our community as it was the last of the "old time" radio shows to originate from the "Nation's Station". It was unusual for a person taking a late night stroll around town to miss a word of the program, because you could hear Moon River resonating from almost every home within the village as they were tuned into Moon River.

Listen as the announcer atones, "Please join me for another journey down Moon River - A lazy stream of dreams, where vain desires forget themselves in the loveliness of sleep. Moon River. Enchanted white ribbon twined in the hair of night where nothing is but sleep. Dream on... sleep on... Care will not seek for thee. Float on. Drift on. Moon River, to the sea. Down the valley of a thousand yesterdays flow the bright waters of Moon River. On and down forever flowing... forever waiting to carry you down to the land of forgetfulness, to the kingdom of sleep... to the realms of... Moon River. A lazy stream of dreams, where vain desires forget themselves in the loveliness of sleep. Moon River enchanted white ribbon Twined in the hair of night, where nothing is but sleep. Dream on. Sleep on. Care will not seek for thee. Float on... drift on... Moon River, to the sea."

I miss it still today.

Remembering the Best

He tackled the man and took him to the ground. The rest of the deputies stood by flabbergasted.

Christmas, of course, is a time for traditions. It is a time to share a few old memories, and to join collectively to honor the people and the times we have shared together in the past.

Just before Christmas this past year, I had the opportunity join in honoring past and current members of the Sheriff's Office. Sheriff Ralph Fizer, Jr., had invited the county commissioners to assist him in presenting awards to three Clinton County Sheriff's Office employees as "Officers of the Year" for 2012.

Deputy Jonathan Bailey received the Michael "Mick" McCoy Memorial Award. Communications Officer Mindi Stevens was awarded the Paul Starkey Memorial Award, and Officer Rick Leasher was honored with the William H. Turner Memorial Award.

As Sheriff Fizer called the names, I sat back in my chair; and as former sheriff, reflected how Mick McCoy, Bill Turner, and Paul Starkey were much more than just names on a plaque. They were men who served Clinton County with courage, sharing a lifelong interest in the welfare of others.

As we looked around the room, we saw the pride on the faces of the young men and women of the Sheriff's Department. Law enforcement is a tough job. All understand there are times when an officer must, as we did a few years ago, "Say a quick prayer, adjust our bulletproof vests, and after a few deep breaths, open the door and walk warily inside."

Deputy Sheriff Mick McCoy was a delightful man. Although he originally pursued the family business, Mick decided to forgo the oil business to follow his passion - law enforcement.

One afternoon Mick and several other deputies arrived at a farm outside Clarksville to serve a court order committing a man to a mental health facility in Cincinnati for an evaluation. With each passing moment, the man became increasingly agitated and resistant. He was also holding a hammer. Out of range of the man, the deputies held a brief conference. They decided they would first divert his attention, then rush and handcuff him. One of the deputies said, "I am going to engage the man in conversation. You guys count to ten and then rush him." The deputy went over to the man ready to begin a conversation with him. After the count of two, Deputy McCoy, a towering, fearless figure rushed forward like an offside linebacker. He tackled the man and took him to the ground. The rest of the deputies stood by flabbergasted. "I guess I jumped off-sides!" Mick laughed.

Dispatcher Paul Starkey began his law enforcement career in Sabina as a member of the Sabina Auxiliary Police and Firemen Association. Paul was always a relaxed and friendly man with a deep baritone voice, perfectly suited for police dispatching. Paul joined the Clinton County Sheriff's Office under Sheriff Don Osborn and remained there through the administration of Sheriff Ralph Fizer, Sr. Paul was known for his calm, resolute presence over the police radio even when dispatching deputies to the most serious calls. He was a dependable and trustworthy officer.

Lieutenant William (Bill) Turner served with the Clinton County Sheriff's Office for many years as a road deputy, and later as a corrections administrator. Born near New Vienna, in Gist Settlement, Bill was an outstanding athlete at New Vienna High School. He carried that same dedication into his position of deputy sheriff and spent many extra hours coordinating prisoner visitations with inmates and their families. Although serving as a corrections supervisor, he was always one of the first deputies to respond during dangerous situations.

The evolution of the Clinton County Sheriff's Office from the Sheriff Don Osborn era to until today has been relatively dramatic and swift in terms of governmental change. It has been a time of steady advancement and modernization.

Sheriff Osborn was appointed sheriff in 1963. He had previously served as a sergeant with the Wilmington Post of the Ohio State Highway Patrol. Prior to his arrival, Clinton County Deputy Sheriffs wore civilian clothes. During his tenure, Don outfitted deputies in uniforms and began utilizing marked sheriff's cruisers.

Sheriff Dallas Kratzer, also a former Ohio State Highway Patrol trooper, replaced Sheriff Osborn in 1976. Dallas worked hard to modernize the office, and brought greater sophistication to its operation. Sheriff Kratzer was a true leader and inspiration.

Ralph Fizer, Sr. was elected Sheriff in 1988. Sheriff Fizer continued to grow and professionalize the Sheriff's Department over the years. Ralph had strong experience earlier as an investigator within the department. He had the innate ability to talk with people, and an unrelenting determination to work cases until they were resolved.

Current Sheriff Ralph Fizer, Jr. replaced his father as sheriff in 2002. He has taken law enforcement in Clinton County to a different level with his progressive leadership. He has stressed teamwork during his tenure as sheriff, and understands these awards represent a wonderful tradition that recognizes teamwork and cohesiveness within the Sheriff's Office.

Susan Lieberman said, "Traditions counter alienation and confusion. They help us define who we are; they provide something steady, reliable, and safe in a confusing world."

Good words to live by.

They Gently Traded Her the Flag for Her Son

As they stepped onto the front porch, Patrick Dwyer's mother walked to the doorway wiping her hands on her apron.

There are certain rituals within families handed down from generation to generation.

One such tradition within our family centers around Election Day. Every election day my mother would ask, "You're planning to vote, aren't you?" I would always answer, "Yes, I am going to vote." Mom even reminded me to vote after I had run for election and was elected to office for the first time, in 1980. She wanted to take no chances.

Mom passed away several years ago, but her reminders still come to mind each Election Day.

Mom never failed to recount a story about one of my cousins, Patrick Dwyer, who had died in 1944 while defending our country fighting in Normandy. I remember her telling me, "There are many worthwhile reasons to vote in every election. Voting is a right, a privilege and a responsibility. Every vote matters. The people we elect affect our country, safety, freedoms, and money. There are some things in life worth fighting for, and voting is one of them. Soldiers have died so you can vote."

What I didn't know until a few years ago is that my older brother, Jack, had been at the Dwyer residence at the time the family received word of Patrick's death.

Jack told me the story of the young man who had lived on the family farm not far away in Wilson Township. Patrick Dwyer had never been outside of the county until he was drafted into the Army during World War II.

Jack said he was about six years old at the time, and happened to be visiting the Dwyer farm. He saw a shiny black car pull into the barnyard, and heard one of our cousins say, "Oh, no." Two Army officers then exited the vehicle and made their way to where the two young boys were standing. The Army officers asked if the parents of Patrick Dwyer were at home.

"Yes, Mom is in the house."

As they stepped onto the front porch, Patrick Dwyer's mother walked to the doorway wiping her hands on her apron. Jack saw her face turn ashen, as he looked-up from the yard to hear one of the officers say, "Mrs. Dwyer, if I may, I have a letter to read to you."

"At the request of the President of the United States, Franklin D. Roosevelt, I regretfully write to inform you that the Purple Heart has been awarded to your son, Private Patrick Joseph Dwyer, who sacrificed his life in defense of his country. We profoundly appreciate the greatness of your loss, for truly the loss ... in this battle for our country ... is a loss by all of us. When the medal reaches you, I want you to know that with it goes our sincere sympathy and the hope that time and the victory of our cause will finally lighten the burden of your grief. Sincerely, Secretary of War, Henry L. Stratton."

The young officers then gave Mrs. Dwyer a crisp salute, turned and walked off the porch. Within those few moments, our family was changed forever. Even sixty-eight years after Patrick's death, I still think about his sacrifice when Election Day comes around.

Just the other day I heard a song on the radio that further reminded me of the Dwyer story.

> *They fold up the stars and the stripes for his mother,*
> *And gently trade her the flag for her son;*
> *A harder exchange never took place in our country,*
> *But it's not the first time it's ever been done.*

These hard exchanges have not been made for the first time by those within our country. Many mothers across America have had to trade their sons for our flag. Mrs. Dwyer traded her son for a flag.

So others could vote.

The Duke, Old Yeller and Me

John Wayne walks away, alone, into the rough country of Monument Valley.

There is nothing that beats a good movie. I remember seeing Frank Capra's, *It's A Wonderful Life*, and a variety of classics like *The Ten Commandments*, *Gone With the Wind*, *Casablanca*, *The Maltese Falcon*, as well as, *Planet of the Apes*, *Goldfinger* and *Davy Crockett*.

A film that made a lasting impression was John Ford's *The Searchers*. The movie begins with a cabin door opening into the desert, and ends with the reunited family walking back through the door as John Wayne walks away, alone, into the rough country of Monument Valley.

In between those scenes, John Wayne had rescued his niece, Debbie, from the Comanche and took her back home.

Much like the opening of the doors in *The Searchers* scenes, the welcoming doors of the Murphy Theatre often opened for my sister, Rita, and me. We remember how we quietly slipped into our seats, and relaxed as time began to slow down. Gone were the worries of the day as we began to enter the worlds of the actors on screen, vicariously sharing their stories.

Most know the background of the Murphy Theatre. Chicago Cubs owner Charles Murphy opened the wonderful showplace for his beloved Clinton County in 1918. Charlie Fischer played the piano at the silent films. Over the years, everything from silent movies to Ricky Nelson graced this historic stage.

My father even told me that as a young boy he had met the Three Stooges after a vaudeville matinee at the Murphy. According to my dad, the Stooges were appearing at the Murphy for three shows. He said he saw them and passed them on the sidewalk as they walked downtown on South South Street to find a sandwich before the evening show. My dad said all three were friendly and spoke as he walked by. He said he was surprised by the short stature of the trio, impressed by Moe's polite and courteous manner, and caught off guard by Curly's shyness. He also said that Larry's hair looked like a haystack gone awry.

Reaching back in time, I remember one particular Saturday afternoon when Rita suggested we go see *Old Yeller*. People enjoy the occasional good cry, especially in a movie theater. But at the age of nine, I wasn't quite ready for *Old Yeller*.

The story unfolded as a young man was made man-of-the-house when his father left home on a cattle drive. The boy found a dog and named him 'Old Yeller'. Both he and his younger brother befriended the dog. The dog was likable but mischievous, stealing food and knocking over pots and pans. At one point, as a rabid wolf approaches the boys, Old Yeller attacked and killed the wolf saving their lives. Having been bitten during the attack, shortly thereafter, Old Yeller's behavior radically began to change. Within a few days, he even turned on the boys, snarling with his canine teeth shown and foaming at the mouth. The older boy was faced with a decision that would be difficult for an adult. Ultimately, as the man-of-the-house, the boy was forced to put Old Yeller to sleep.

All I remember when the credits began to roll is that I was still stuck in my seat. The lights came on and I sat there as if in a daze, devastated by what had transpired onscreen. I was crying. My sister was crying. The people next to us were crying. It seemed almost everyone in the theatre was crying.

Over the years, I wondered why the movie had made me feel so sad. Then I understood. The scene with Old Yeller reflected real life. Real life isn't always made-up of happy endings, but is often seasoned with reality, and having to make tough decisions for the greater good.

A few weeks later, we saw reality again on the screen as *The Searchers* ended, and John Wayne picked-up Natalie Wood and tenderly said, "Let's go home, Debbie."

They went home. And in a sense, we do, too, every time we visit the beloved Murphy - a home that keeps guard over our most cherished childhood memories.

And to some of the very best times of our lives.

Saying Good-bye to Traditional Restraints

The change, like most change, came slowly. At first, the curse words on television were like a dripping faucet - one word, then another, and then another. As time went on, the curse words became more frequent and distasteful.

Unfortunately, no one fixed the drip.

These weren't new words, of course, but we didn't hear them often. Before long, we heard those same words more and more frequently around our little town. Those words were like seeds. Many believe that the seeds for the decline were sewn during the decade of the 1960s when a sea change occurred in American society.

We also saw a certain coarseness emerging within our culture.

A few years ago, I was on a motorcycle trip and came across a small country church nestled high in the mountains of West Virginia. Inside, up near the altar, was a book where parishioners and visitors wrote petitions asking for God's intercession with their burdens and trials. A thin elderly woman came in the side door and spent several minutes writing in the book. After she left, I walked over and opened the book. "We pray for the strength to resist and overcome the multitude of evils that have been allowed to grow in our culture once traditional restraints were removed," the woman had written.

Her words were profound. True, and yet so sad. The restraints she was talking about were personal virtues, and self-control. Restraints dripping away like the water from a leaky faucet.

Recently, my wife and I went to a Cincinnati Reds game. The profanity, within clear earshot of my wife, was extraordinary. There were several groups of clean-cut young people sitting behind us. We have all seen the pose many times. The beer can held proudly, about waist high, like a badge of courage for the world to see. As the game went on the beer continued to flow. We heard curse words beginning to drip like a beer spigot with a loose fitting. There was no redeeming value to those words - only shock value.

Profanity adds to the depth of coarseness in society. It is the language of aggression - often the precursor to violence. I've seen it often in law enforcement.

Suddenly, there was a commotion a few rows down from us. First, we heard a woman cuss her boyfriend. Then, her boyfriend cussed back. Within a minute, a boy who couldn't have been much older than eight or nine cussed the boyfriend. The people holding the beer cans behind us began to laugh and cheer. Brenda and I left the game.

The coarseness in our society seems unrestrained. The steady bombardment of shocking behavior, language, dress, rudeness, and violence desensitizes us. There seems to be no respect or sense of consideration for others. We see speeding and reckless operation almost every day on our highways and streets. The parking lots at Wal-Mart and Kroger's are becoming more dangerous. We see careless, impatient drivers driving much too fast and with complete disregard for the welfare of others.

We confront this rudeness on a daily basis on television, radio, and computer games. Some blogs allows 'Skip from Kansas' to hide behind a fictitious name to insult and belittle others. Unlike *Cheers*, "Where everybody knows your name," no one knows this person's name. What purpose does hiding behind a shield of anonymity serve, other than to embolden the writer to say things he or she might not say if they were using their real name, just to create a stir and get a strong reaction?

This adds more coarseness to society.

Maybe we see more incivility today because we are forgetting that we need each other. Maybe we think we are teaching our children respect, but perhaps the computer, TV and movies are countering our efforts to teach how to embrace a life tempered with patience, grace, gratitude, compassion and a gentle willingness to cede to others.

Maybe we need to pay more attention to our children and

spend as much time looking into their eyes as we do facing a television or computer screen.

Maybe my dad got it right. During the 39 years of life we shared together, I never heard my dad utter one curse word, nor ever take the name of our Lord in vain. Not once. Maybe it was because every night of his life, I remembered that he turned down his bed, knelt on his knees beside it, and asked his Creator for the grace to better serve his fellow man.

Maybe, just maybe, traditional restraints were not such a bad thing after all.

The Psalm Singers from Cleveland

Frankly, I don't know what my son was doing in the chapel in the first place.

Thursday, March 26, 1970, will forever remain stamped into the memories of Mrs. Dora Dellaria and Mrs. Louise Honor. The women, from Parma, Ohio and Fairview Park, Ohio, respectively, were conducting Christian Science services in the Cuyahoga Jail Chapel just before 3:30 in the afternoon. The chapel was alive, filled with friendly greetings, a little singing, and redeeming prayer.

Suddenly, an inmate stopped Mrs. Honor in mid-prayer. "Ladies, I have a gun. It would be best if you both join me and my two friends as we all walk out together," an inmate whispered to the two Psalm singers. "Walk very slowly in front us," he added, as the women became walking shields.

"Looks like we'd better go with these gentlemen, Dora," Louise said as she turned toward the door, her heart pounding so loud she was afraid her friend would hear it.

As this improbable group walked unimpeded through one door after another, the Cuyahoga

County Sheriff met them on the front steps of the jail."Give me the keys to your cruiser, Sheriff," one of the inmates demanded.

"No, I won't do that. You can take the cruiser from the Warrensville Heights Police Department, though" the sheriff generously responded.

"That will work," the prisoner said as he jumped into the cruiser. As he adjusted his seat, his hand brushed across a shotgun - primed and loaded. He also found a sheriff's hat in the back seat. Within a few seconds, the inmate put on the hat, blasted the siren, and started south on Interstate 71 at a high rate of speed.

Gathering his senses, the sheriff called the prisoners over the police radio. He asked the men to release the women. "We will drop them off on the outskirts of Cleveland," the driver in the hat responded. They didn't stop.

Within minutes, the FBI and U.S. Marshals took control of the escape since the inmates were federal prisoners. The agents gave strict orders to local law enforcement: "We are going to give the escapees a free pass through Ohio because they have 'promised us' they will release their hostages when they get to their intended destination in Tennessee," the federal agents ordered the flabbergasted Ohio police.

As the chase proceeded south, nearly every sheriff's office along the way added a few more cruisers to the pursuit along the way. The chase, reaching speeds of 100-mph, soon took on a carnival-like atmosphere. In fact, the chase of O.J. Simpson paled in comparison.

On the outskirts of Wilmington, I was riding in a Clinton County Sheriff's cruiser as a young 'ride-a-long' with Deputy Sheriff Larry Newland. "Why don't we ride out to 68 and 71?" Larry asked. "They should be coming through Clinton County in about an hour."

Within forty minutes, we saw the entourage. There were close to sixty police cruisers with lights blazing following the escapees as they zoomed south on 71. "Let's get in the chase, Larry," I said as the whizzing posse sped past.

"We better not. Don wouldn't like it," Larry said referring to then Sheriff Don Osborne. "He doesn't like us to be on the Interstate."

As luck would have it, or in this case, as bad luck would have it for the escapees, Colonel Leslie Pyles of the Kentucky State Police had been listening to the chase on the radio.

As the pursuit approached Kentucky, the FBI ordered the Kentucky State Police to stay out of the way. Colonel Pyles, a man with a strong sense of right and wrong, had other ideas. He immediately radioed back, "If you fellas want to talk to these crooks, then keep them in Ohio. If they come to Kentucky, we are going to arrest them."

At that point, as they say in sports, the momentum shifted.

The caravan entered Kentucky in Covington and continued south on Interstate 75. Within forty minutes, the long trail of flashing lights approached Georgetown, Kentucky. The escapee who was driving and still wearing the sheriff's hat, was shouting through the loudspeaker, "Get out of my way!"

Suddenly, just like lightening from a restless summer storm, fifty or more Kentucky State Police cruisers snapped on their brilliant flashing blue lights in unison. Simultaneously, a shotgun roared. A state police sharpshooter riding alongside the stolen cruiser had shot a hole in its front tire. Just as quickly as the chase began, the chase ended.

The bizarre pursuit had covered 19 counties and 339 miles, and had lasted seven hours. As it turned out, the gun used by the escapees used was a fake. In fact, the 'gun' had been carved from a bar of Ivory soap.

Later, as news of the capture filtered back to Cleveland, the mother of one of the escapees visited one of the female victims, Mrs. Dellaria. "I am sorry for what happened," the tearful mother said. "Frankly, I don't know what my son was doing in the chapel in the first place. He isn't a Christian Scientist, we raised him Methodist," she sniffed as she walked through the steel door never looking back.

The Man at
St. John's Church

He might have just been a gifted storyteller who happened along that day.

Brenda and I lived and worked in Richmond, Virginia, a town rich in history, for a few years.

On the east end of town sitting atop a hill in one of Richmond's oldest neighborhoods, Church Hill, was St. John's Episcopal Church. Still active, it was built in 1741.

One evening after work, Brenda and I decided to walk the three blocks up to the famous church where Patrick Henry gave his "Give me liberty or give me death!" speech. As we arrived, a reenactment of the famous speech had just taken place. It was quite impressive and dramatic.

There were several performers standing around in period costumes waiting for the crowd to disperse. Brenda and I decided we would take a break, too. We crossed the street to a nice city park, and sat on a bench under the trees waiting for the hustle and bustle to settle down at the church.

We returned to the church and found the only person still there was an elderly African American gentleman lumbering about. We thought he might have been the caretaker of the church waiting to lock-up. He was friendly, starting-up a conversation asking us where we lived. We explained where we lived, and then in turn, asked him if he lived in Richmond as well. He laughed and said quietly, "Not only have I lived all of my life in Richmond, my family has been here since before the American Revolution."

Seeming to be in no hurry, we started walking around the church, and the old man joined us. He said that he worked for the parish doing odd jobs and such, and that in fact, he had come to the church almost every day of his life with the exception of "the day it snowed three inches". "That's a big deal in the South. We couldn't go anywhere because of the snow," he laughed.

"One of my ancestors, a slave, took care of the horses during the Second Virginia Convention right over there," he pointed. He said his family had always talked about how George Washington, Richard Henry Lee, Thomas Jefferson and other important people arrived in their carriages, went into St. John's Parish, and decided to unite against British rule once-and-for- all. "It was a turning point for America."

"My daddy talked about how his father, my grandfather, had told the story how our ancestor stood outside talking with Patrick Henry, as he smoked a pipe, before going into the church."

"According to my family, Patrick Henry rode-up on horseback and dismounted just over by that tree," the man said. The elder gentleman seemed sad for some reason. "Back then, we never started a conversation with white gentlemen unless we were spoken to first," he continued.

"Mr. Henry was saddened by his ride to Richmond because he had passed the church where he and his wife had been married," he continued.

"We had a wonderful family and a wonderful life together, but my wife was sick and couldn't recover," Mr. Henry told my ancestor. "I watched over her as she died at home, just a month ago. It is very hard for me for me to be here today. I didn't feel like making the ride to Richmond, but our cause is so important. We must break away from the British."

"Please excuse my dust. I just planted a lilac tree next to her grave this morning," the man said Mr. Henry had told his cousin.

"'And don't you know, they say that tree is still there today," the man told Brenda and me. "Just a few steps away from the house."

"According to our family lore, it was just a few minutes later Mr. Henry walked into St. John's Church and delivered his famous speech, "Is life so dear, or peace so sweet, as to be purchased at the price of chains and slavery? Forbid it, Almighty God! I know not what course others may take; but as for me, Give me Liberty, or give me Death!"

"The people who came to this church that day were no different from you and me. They had families, personal problems and jobs, and they had a lot to lose by taking on the British Crown," he ended.

To this day, we do not know if the stories the man shared with us about his ancestor and Patrick Henry were true or not. He might have just been a gifted storyteller who happened along that day, but we do know he held us spellbound for over an hour. True or not, it just felt good to hear the stories.

Two-hundred and thirty-seven years later, we still hear talk of America losing its liberties. On this Independence Day, maybe it's time we stood-up, too.

Happy Fourth of July!

Eugene: The Stone Man with the Golden Smile

Somewhere in America, maybe in a city nearby, a man went missing in 1929, never to return home.

Times were tough in the summer of 1929 as the Great Depression was dawning on the cities and farms of America, forcing thousands of people to leave their homes in an effort to find work.

It was late spring and unusually hot on June 6, 1929, when John Phelps, the local superintendent of the Sabina Water and Electric Plant, sat down on his front porch. As Mr. Phelps relaxed, he couldn't help but notice a black man, about fifty to sixty years old slowly walking east past his house on Washington Street in Sabina. "That man might be sick," Mr. Phelps thought to himself, but a stranger walking through small towns in the Midwest wasn't unusual at that time. As the economy worsened the number of homeless, then commonly referred to as hoboes, increased proportionately. They were riding the rails, and Sabina was a railroad town.

The next day, Gus J. Miller, the Clinton County Sherriff at the time, sped through Sabina at a high rate of speed eastbound on SR 22 and 3.

Within a few minutes, the county coroner, Dr. C.E. Kinzel, passed by heading in the same direction. Finally, the village residents noticed a hearse from Littleton's Funeral Home slowly leave town.

News quickly spread that the body of the African-American man seen earlier walking along the sidewalk, was found slumped against a fence post on the old 3C Highway about .07 tenths of a mile from Borum Road. His body lay just in front of a small pond near an old schoolhouse as if he had fallen asleep.

Many who grew up in Clinton County know the story. Law enforcement attempted to identify the man with no success. Finally, in desperation, authorities decided to place Eugene's body in a small brick building behind Littletons, which still stands today, in hopes that someone might identify him.

As the sheriff searched the dead man's body, he found a small slip of paper with the words 1118 Yale Avenue, Cincinnati, Ohio, printed neatly across the top, $1.41 in change, and a gold ring with the initial 'E' in the middle. The man wore the ring on his middle finger because he was missing fingers on both hands.

Sheriff Miller drove to Cincinnati and met with Cincinnati Police detectives. Their hopes vanished when they drove to the address not too far from the old Crosley Field, only to find a vacant lot. They knocked at the door of the home nearest to the lot. "Sir, do you know a black man from this area who may be missing," the sheriff asked the owner of the home, Eugene

Johnson.

"No, I have no knowledge of a missing man from this neighborhood, and I don't remember ever seeing anyone matching the description of the dead body in your county," he added.

Returning to Clinton County and lacking a name for the deceased, the coroner and sheriff decided to call the man "Eugene."

Sheriff Miller transferred the body to Littleton's Funeral Home to have it embalmed. Days went by, then weeks and months. No missing persons reports were received that matched "Eugene's" description.

"Let's go see Eugene!" my Dad said one Saturday afternoon while our family was visiting in Sabina.

"Oh, Bob, let's not! He will scare the boys," I heard my Mom reply.

The year was 1953. I was only five years old and my brother Kevin was three when the idea struck my Dad. Regardless, we were not alone. People came from all around to view the "man of stone". It wasn't long before we were walking the two blocks down Jackson Street toward Littleton's Funeral Home.

"Eugene" as he lay in repose, was well-dressed in a charcoal-colored suit, with a white shirt and a tie. His clean and fresh clothes, which the Littleton's changed every six months, took me aback. His skin looked a slate gray, and he had rather large incisors, two front teeth encased in gold. He had a rather serene look of composure on his face. I remember touching his face and feeling the "man of stone".

As a former sheriff the mysterious death of "Eugene" had always intrigued me. Several years ago, I decided to do a bit of investigating on my own. Although the coroner had not conducted an autopsy, there was a death certificate on file that listed 'natural causes' as the cause of death. The Littleton's had noted at the time of the embalming that the man had several old stab wounds on his body.

For many years, and until case law changed the practice, it wasn't unusual for those down-on-their-luck to stop in towns and ask to sleep in the local jail overnight. Those individuals were nicknamed 'sleepers' by law enforcement.

With this thought in mind, I traveled to the Highland, Fayette, Greene, Montgomery, and Warren County jails with the hope of finding a prisoner or 'sleeper' recorded on the jail blotter matching "Eugene's" unique description. Surprisingly, the records were available for those years, but after scouring the logs for hours; unfortunately, there was no match.

It is hard to say if the mystery surrounding "Eugene" will ever be solved. It is something that intrigues me still to this day, a man who went missing eighty-four years ago, and ending-up in Clinton County. The odds may be insurmountable, but one thing we know for sure is that somewhere in America, maybe in a city nearby, a man went missing in 1929, never to return home. Perhaps a mother lost a son, a family lost a father, or a wife lost a husband on that fateful day in June as he took his last rest upside a fencepost just outside of Sabina.

As Proverbs 22.1 says, "A good name is more desirable than great riches; to be esteemed is better than silver or gold." So far, his good name was taken with him to the grave.

Ashland, Virginia

More Civil War battles were fought within this 75-mile radius than on any other piece of land anywhere.

One of my favorite places in the whole world is Ashland, Virginia. It's a quaint little town where the railroad tracks run through the middle of the downtown, and the residents love it that way.

I first visited Ashland in 1993 while traveling for the Virginia Department of Probation and Parole. I had made my egress from Interstate 95 at the Ashland exit to eat lunch at a picturesque downtown diner. The summer day was bright and warm, so I decided to take a walk around to the see the local sights. Much to my surprise, I saw a small train station sitting alongside two railroad tracks that ran directly through the middle of town. What a scenic town, I thought to myself. As a train fancier, I decided to walk around and further explore the area.

Affectionately known by local residents as the "Center of the Universe" for its central location within the state, Ashland is located in the heart of Hanover County, Virginia. Developed by the railroad as a mineral springs resort, the origin of the town dates back to the late 1840's. Officially incorporated on February 19, 1858, the town was named "Ashland" after native son Henry Clay's estate in Kentucky.

With the relocation of Randolph Macon College to Ashland in 1868, the town evolved from a railroad resort to a small college town. Ashland was a town born of the railroad, and it was obvious the townspeople were proud of their history. The town is a diverse collection of neighborhoods and businesses, with a blend of architectural styles of large Victorian homes.

As I continued my stroll, I discovered the area to be rich in history. The railroad, which was operated by the old Richmond, Fredericksburg, and Potomac Railroad Company, was at one time a pivotal prize during the Civil War. More important, more Civil War battles were fought within this 75-mile radius than on any other piece of land anywhere within the nation.

I stopped at a small "mom-and-pop" grocery store along the main street, much like Sanders Market in Port William, Ohio where I had grown up. The elderly proprietor told me his grandfather had told him he had personally seen Lee's wary Army of Confederates march southward along the railroad tracks, the same tracks that lay just outside his doors today.

The grocer said his grandfather recalled that they "marched in such deep silence that a man with his eyes shut would only have known that anyone was on the road by the occasional rattle of a canteen." Places like the Wilderness, Spotsylvania, and North Anna lay behind them. Cold Harbor, Petersburg, Richmond and ten more months of war lay ahead," he said.

As I stepped outside from the grocery store, I heard a train's whistle in the distance. I knew it was approaching Ashland because of the Doppler effect, which is a variable pitch observed in the whistle of a locomotive as it approaches and then recedes. My hunch was soon proven correct, as an Amtrak passenger train slowly wound its way through the main street of town, hurrying along on its journey to the big city of Washington, D.C.

My pleasant visit ended as casually as it had begun. I quietly walked to my car to begin my journey home – home to another lovely town, Staunton, Virginia; to tell my wife, Brenda, of my new-found treasure.

Grandfather William Haley

My sister Rita found a written note Grandfather William Haley had left after his death that mentioned the famous people he had seen during his lifetime. The list included: President Harry S. Truman, Mrs. Bess Truman, Miss Margaret Truman, President Franklin Roosevelt, Eleanor Roosevelt, President Warren G. Harding, Babe Ruth, Efan Booth, Salvation Army, Abram J. Ryan, William Jennings Bryan, General J. W. Denver, Orville Wright, Marcus Loew, Fats Waller, Mark Hanna, Newton Baker, Secretary of War during WWI, John Free, Governor Foraker, Governor Campbell, Governor Bushnell, Governor Cox, Governor Harmon, Governor Frank Hanley, Governor Frank Lausche, Elbert Hubbard, Charles Ebbetts, Charles W. Murphy, John L. Sullivan, and Jo Jo the Dog Faced Boy, plus baseball, stage ad radio stars galore.

Things That Don't Happen Every Day!

One Head is Better Than None

In 1881, I saw Mrs. John Denehy carry a bucket of milk in each hand, and one on top of her head!

How High's the Water, Mama?

In 1907, when our family lived on the Reardon place, I was driving home in a road-wagon, and my son, Joe, aged four, was with me. The creek was high and spread over its bank, but I thought I could get through. When the wagon got to the middle of the creek, the water came high on the horse's sides, and raised the wagon-bed up. The streaming water did not clear the standards, but lifted up the front end and the front bolster, coupling pin and all. The end of the coupling pole was split, and I fixed it with a small bolt with a small square heard. That bolt-head prevented the pole from coming out. If it had loosened, the back part of the wagon would have stayed in the creek and Joe and I would have floated downstream. The Luck of the Irish!

You Can Lead a Horse to Water

One Saturday evening in 1882, my Father turned our main horse out to pasture. Shortly thereafter, he put a three-year-old mare that he planned to drive the next day, inside the pen. As Dad opened the gate to let the other horse out to drink, the mare ran out of the barn neighing, and made for the gate about 250 feet away. She went at it as hard as she could run, and sailed over the gate without touching the gate that was about five-and-a-half-feet high.
That was one horse in a hurry.

The Comet

The same year, I saw a very fine comet. No, it wasn't the Haley Comet!

The Trouble With Trees

In the 1890's, I sawed and chopped a tree completely through, and it did not fall. The tree was two-feet-and-a-half thick.

In addition, in the 1892, I saw a large spreading elm tree fall, with not a breath of air stirring. The weather was extremely hot at the time.

Hard Snow

On another occasion, I saw snowdrifts so hard that horses walked on top of them and stepped over the fences.

Horses are Hard to Figure Out

In about 1908, I was planning to let the horse, Rob Roy, outside the main pen one evening to graze on some grass. Rob Roy seeing the gate open made for the road and took the other horses with him. He ran down the road and across the fields, and stopped about three miles away. I went after him, brought him and the rest of the horses with me, and put them in the barn.

Then in the gloaming, I walked in behind them, and Rob Roy, knowing that he was in for a smacking, let fly with both feet and nicked my coat. No Harm Done!

Get A Horse

One Saturday night in 1917 or 1918, we were coming home from town, Bernadette, myself and a full load of kids. As we started to turn-off Locust Street onto High Street, there was the roar of a speeding car going at 60-miles-per-hour and running on the wrong side of the street. I stopped our car and the speeding car nicked our front fender—ting, ting—and roared on down the street. No Harm Done!

A Little Girl and a Pig

The year was 1926, and one evening I was in the barn milking when my daughter, Rosemary, age 4, came in. As she was walking through the barn, she fell and instantly an old sow jumped on her. Rosemary screamed, and I came running. I grabbed a single-tree that was leaning against a post. The sow was holding Rosemary down with one foot and was tearing at her chest. I brought the single-tree down on the sow's back as hard as I could. That made her let go and run away. Rosemary's chest was bruised, but otherwise she was all right. But supposed I hadn't been there. You said it – The Luck of the Irish!

The Weasel and the Shotgun

One day when we lived on Henry Speer's place, a hen and weasel caused us concern. A hen made a big fuss on the back orchard, and I grabbed the gun and ran out. A weasel had caught a baby chicken, dragged it to a pile of boards, and was tugging at it trying to get it through a crack at a distance of eight feet.... I shot the weasel to pieces and it did not injure the chicken at all.

Still excited, I leaned the gun against the fence and held the weasel up. My wife, Bernadette, was by me, and, bang went the gun's other barrel under my left arm, so close that the concussion made me feel like I'd been socked.

"I didn't know it was loaded," said my son Joe, age 4.

Digging a Well

In 1903, at the place down the road where we started housekeeping, I was digging a well. I was down twelve feet, when someone got too close to the top of the well and a large rock fell into the well. I was in a stooping position, and the rock missed me by at least three inches. No Harm Done!

William Haley's 'Luck-of-the-Irish' thoughts.

Famous People
I Have Seen

In keeping with family tradition, I'd like to include here the famous people I have seen

In keeping with family tradition, I'd like to include here the famous people I have seen: Johnny Mathis, Smiley Burnett, Tony Randall-Stringbean-Peter, Paul and Mary-Merle Haggard-James Taylor-Hank Snow-Little Jimmy Dickens-Grandpa Jones-David Brinkley-Elizabeth Dole-Tom T. Hall-Eddy Arnold-Whispering Bill Anderson-Reba McIntire-Roy Clark-Ernest Tubb-Tex Ritter-Jesse Jackson-Tammy Wynette-George Jones-Crystal Gayle-Reba-Dolly Parton-Barbara Mandrell-Hulk Hogan-Ricky Nelson-William Rehnquist-Linda Ronstadt-Marty Robbins-Pat Boone-Ted Turner-George Steinbrenner-Emmy Lou Harris-Ray Combs-Nick Clooney-Bob Braun-Gene Autry-June Carter Cash-Michael Jordan-Ernie Banks-First Lady Barbara Bush-Cloris Leachman-Dean Jones-Lefty McFadden-Bo Bo Brazil-Jonathan Winters-Glen Campbell-Johnny Cash-the Statler Brothers-Ted Kluzewski-Vada Pinson-Frank Robinson-Pete Rose-Johnny Bench-Stan Musial-Willie Mays-Bob Cousy-Oscar Robertson-Bill

Russell-John Glenn-Chet Atkins-Minnie Pearl-Roy Acuff-Jimmy
Dean-Joe E. Lewis-Nosey the Clown-President Ronald Reagan-
President George W. Bush-President George W. H. Bush-Uncle
Al and Captain Wendy-President Richard Nixon-President
Jimmy Carter-Vice President Al Gore-Sweet Daddy Siki-Bob
Hope-George Allen-President Gerald Ford-Paul Brown-Virginia
Governor Jim Gilmore-Robert Conrad-Don Knotts-Perry Como-
Richard Harris-Senator Bob Dole-Senator Ted Kennedy-Uncle
Orrie-President Bill Clinton-Jack Palance-Alabama·Governor
George Wallace-Hank Aaron-Neil Armstrong-Larry Bird-
Mac Wiseman-Brenda Lee-Larry Moles-Joe Nuxhall-Marty
Brennaman-Englebert Humperdink-Jim and Jesse and the
Virginia Boys.

Presidents of the United States

My encounter with President Nixon in 1974 was the first time I
had met a United States president. It wouldn't be the last.

In 1976, while in Columbus, Ohio, I met then President Gerald
Ford, as well as, his running mate, Senator Majority Leader Bob
Dole, in Clinton County, Ohio. I had the opportunity to shake the
hands of both men. During the summer of 1976, I saw President
Jimmy Carter in Columbus, Ohio working the crowds on Broad
Street.

During my campaign for Clinton County Sheriff in 1980,
I traveled to Columbus with a group of Clinton County
Republicans where I saw presidential candidate, President Ronald
Reagan. Robert Conrad of *Wild, Wild West* fame accompanied

Reagan. As they walked directly past where I was standing, I had the opportunity to shake hands with the future president.

In April 1982, I had the opportunity to see President Ronald Reagan once again – this time in Cincinnati. Later that month, I saw President George H.W. Bush at the Ohio Theater in Columbus. After the Reagan years ended, I saw Vice-President Dan Qualye in Columbus. I had my picture taken with First Lady Barbara Bush in Richmond, Virginia, years later when Brenda and I lived there.

Then presidential candidate, Bill Clinton and his wife, Hillary Clinton, while on the campaign trail along with Vice-presidential candidate Al Gore and his wife, Tipper, stopped in Wilmington, Ohio at the courthouse. Both candidates spoke and were in town well over an hour. Mr. Clinton wanted to visit Clinton County because of the name similarity while on his bus tour from New York to Arkansas.

Brenda and I had the opportunity to see President George W. Bush "up-close-and- personal" during the Gilmore years in Richmond, Virginia, as well.

Virginia Governor Jim Gilmore was the host for a major fundraiser for Presidential Candidate George W. Bush at the Jefferson Hotel, a magnificent Richmond landmark. Built in 1895, the Jefferson Hotel has been recognized as one of the grandest hotels in America. Adding to the prestigious occasion was the fact that tickets for the event had sold for one-thousand dollars apiece, which had limited the number of guests to the wealthy and influential. Brenda and I were able to attend the grand affair, because we had volunteered to serve as ushers to assist the Republican Party of Virginia as host and hostess. As the clock struck eight o'clock, George W. Bush and Governor Jim Gilmore walked down the large stairway, which, by the way, has been rumored (wrongly) to have been the stairway where the famous stairway scene in "Gone With the Wind" was filmed. As Governor Gilmore and Texas Governor Bush walked past, Governor Gilmore looked over at me, waved and said, "Hi, Pat, how are you?" We were amazed and a little shocked that out of hundreds of influential people in attendance, the Governor would single me out. I had worked for Governor Gilmore for about six months and during that time he we got to know each other. He always seemed to like some of the stories I told him. I feel very honored that Governor Gilmore gave me a memory that I will cherish for the rest of my life.

As the time neared for us to begin seating the guests and dignitaries, I told Brenda, who is known for her fondness for hugging people, "Whatever you do, please do not try to hug George or Laura. If the Secret Service doesn't take you down, I will."

As an aside, my grandfather William Haley saw Presidents Hoover and Roosevelt; and my mother, Ellen Haley, saw President Kennedy in Dayton, Ohio during the 1960 campaign.

Peaches in His Wheaties

Tom Mitchell, a gifted speaker who was also an FBI agent from the Cincinnati Office, was in great demand at the various law enforcement events within our area. I first heard Tom speak at the Buckeye State Sheriffs' Association, of which I was a member, at their Winter Meeting held at the Marriott Hotel in Columbus, Ohio.

Tom, who was white, told the audience that his parents were southern aristocrats, and that a black mammy in Georgia had raised him. Tom said he remembered that his dad had a favorite peach tree in his front yard. Whenever the young man misbehaved, his mammy would tell his daddy, who then took a switch from the tree and gave his son a whipping. Tom said the morale of the story was: "My daddy thought it was more important to have stripes on my rear end, than peaches with his Wheaties."

When You Wish Upon a Star

I discovered the voice of Jiminy Cricket was provided by a vaudevillian by the name of Cliff Edwards.

Walt Disney was a father figure to many of us who grew up in the fifties. He had a comfortable presence in front of the camera, and I always enjoyed watching "Disneyland" and the "Wonderful World of Disney" as a young boy growing up in Port William.

I remember lying on the living room floor at our home in Port, always within two feet of our black and white television set, watching Walt Disney each week as he introduced the topic for the evening's show. Every week would have a different theme, sometimes the show would be a cartoon like Mickey Mouse or Jiminy Cricket, and sometimes it would be a western like Davy Crockett or Zorro.

Many years later, I discovered the voice of Jiminy Cricket was provided by a vaudevillian by the name of Cliff Edwards. Edwards was also known as "Ukulele Ike".

The amazing element of this story is the fact that Cliff Edwards looks just like Jiminy Cricket! His head is shaped like Jiminy's, and I am sure this physical resemblance did not go unnoticed by Walt Disney. It makes one wonder, which came first - did the studio artists paint Jiminy to look like Ike, or did Walt hire Ike because he looked liked Jiminy Cricket? Whichever, the high note Ike hits at the end of "When You Wish Upon a Star" confirms that Walt made the proper choice.

Jesus Must Have Been with You

Jean Haley is married to my nephew, Tim. Jean had worked for an airline in Cincinnati, Ohio, for many years, and prided herself on her almost perfect attendance. Therefore, it came as no surprise to the family as the radio announced business closings that Jean declared she was driving to her job in Cincinnati. The snow was still falling and conditions were worsening with each passing hour. About forty-five minutes after Jean left home, Tim received a call from the Ohio State Highway Patrol that Jean had been involved in an accident on SR 73 West. Fortunately, she was not injured. Tim and my brother, Jack, arrived at the scene of the accident and found Jean sitting in a patrol cruiser next to her car, which was sitting on its top in a cornfield.

The ride back to Wilmington in Jack's truck was a quiet one. No one spoke for the thirteen miles back to Spring Street. As they approached his house, they noticed the cars in the driveway. Jack's wife, Nancy, had called Tim's brothers, Tony and John, as well as, sisters Amy and Ann, to notify them of Jean's accident. They all had immediately rushed over to their dad and mom's home.

The house was noisy when Jean, Tim, and Jack walked in. However, once it became apparent that Jean was safe, a hush spread over the house. After several minutes, Nancy was the first to break the silence.

"We are so happy you were uninjured. All we can say is that Jesus must have been with you," she said.

No one said anything until Jack, his Irish wit breaking through said, "yeah, and I bet He never rides with her again."

Wrong Way
on Interstate 64

In a matter of seconds, the car sped by, narrowly missing a head-on collision with me.

I had departed from my home in Staunton, Virginia on June 5, 2001, on a business trip heading west on Interstate 64 to Clifton Forge, Virginia. At approximately 11:40 a.m., as I approached the 220 exit ramp for Clifton Forge, I observed a car pull through the median crossover in front of me, and pass me heading east in the westbound lane. The vehicle had headed directly toward me. In a matter of seconds, the car sped by, narrowly missing a head-on collision with me. The driver failed to stop. In fact, the elderly woman driving the wayward vehicle appeared unfazed by the near miss, and continued her journey on the interstate in the wrong direction at a high rate of speed.

Immediately, I called the Virginia State Police and having a law-enforcement background, described the situation to the dispatcher. After I completed my call to the dispatcher, I decided to follow-up and do what I could to help avert a potential tragedy. I exited the westbound interstate and re-entered in the eastbound lane, hoping to gain the attention of the elderly female driver before she struck an unsuspecting motorist. I drove at a high rate of speed in an effort to catch-up to the elderly driver, but after traveling approximately four miles, the lanes diverged and I was unable to see the vehicle.

A short distance later, I once again was able to see the other lane, and caught a glimpse of the speeding car that was still proceeding eastbound in the westbound lane. With no law enforcement officers nearby, I decided at this point that I had to try to stop her. If I didn't get her stopped, no one else would either. I was forced to accelerate, reaching speeds of 90 mph in an attempt to move ahead of the disoriented driver. At approximately the 38-mile marker I saw a crossover. I immediately pulled my car into the crossover. Within a moment, I observed the wayward vehicle heading directly toward me. As the car approached, I noticed several cars and trucks violently swerving to miss the car, in an effort to avert head-on collisions. I quickly parked my vehicle in the crossover and ran onto the highway, to try to gain the confused female driver's attention.

Thankfully, she responded favorably to my hand signals and began to slow down as she approached me, eventually pulling to a complete stop near the median.

It became obvious to me immediately that the driver was, in fact, confused when she asked me why I had flagged her down, and stopped her. When I questioned her as to why she had been driving the wrong way on a major interstate for almost ten miles, she said she had no idea. Thankfully, the driver remained calm and was agreeable with my detaining her until a Virginia State Police Trooper arrived.

Looking back, we were all so fortunate and blessed to have avoided the almost certain tragedy that awaited her and each of the unsuspecting, innocent motorists who ventured near her path.

Farmer Pat

Frank Skidmore had been a Wilmington Police Officer for many years when I joined the force in 1970. In his "off-time", Frank helped his father and brother care for the family farm located on Mad River Road, near Martinsville, Ohio.

One summer, Frank asked me if I would be willing to help him and his family bale hay at the farm. I was 21 years of age and in good physical shape so I told him sure, I would be happy to help them.

I was a city boy with no farming experience. Frank assigned me to work the elevator. The elevator carried the bales to the haymow inside the bright red barn that sat just to the south of the family place.

My duties were to lift the bale from the wagon and place into in the elevator, which would convey it to the top of the barn; where another farmhand was standing by stacking the bales inside the hot loft.

All was going well, until suddenly I fell off the

wagon into the elevator. I was whipped down from the wagon unto the elevator, my shirt caught in the auger. I was slowly carried up the shaft of the 20-foot elevator with no way of escape. I tried pulling myself loose to no avail. Fortunately, when I reached the top of the barn, I was thrown clear of the elevator, landing on a couple of bales of hay uninjured. I could only imagine the surprised look on the farm hand's face when he was expecting a bale of hay only to look up to see a pale Patrick Haley being hurled through the opening of the barn.

Years later, I remember thinking I had been so ignorant of the ways of the farm. Not until the whole experience was over did I realize the true danger.

My ride up the elevator at the Skidmore farm was one of those life experiences that even now at times, causes me to wake-up during the middle of the night with a cold sweat, thinking about my close brush with death. Thankfully, it wasn't my time to die.

Baby Ruth

The man is Gandhi-looking; so thin you can count his ribs.

Years ago, in about 1976, I saw a wall poster at the old G.C. Murphy in Wilmington, Ohio, of an emaciated man obviously marooned on a small island. The man is Gandhi-looking; so thin you can count his ribs. It is obvious he has not eaten in days and is anxiously awaiting a nourishing meal. He is sitting cross-legged on the sand excitedly opening a box marked "Care". When he opens the box, he discovers about 200 Baby Ruth Candy Bars inside.

"In retrospect, I wish I hadn't stubbornly attempted to use the "native tongue" to order dinner," the man thought to himself.

A Toast...
to Babe Hardy

"Stan Laurel
vexed Oliver and
frustrated him and
inflicted physical
havoc upon him
at every turn
in the road.

Sixty years ago, Paul Pumpian gave the
following toast at a Los Angeles meeting in
celebration of Oliver Hardy's birthday.

"If a man was so proud of his honor, dignity
and chivalry that he wore these virtues like
medals-and yet he found that everywhere he
went there were people waiting to strip these
things from him, you'd have a very tragic
character."

"That is, unless that individual was Oliver
Norvell Hardy - the man who took his own
genuine sense of honor and dignity and chivalry
to the screen, and exaggerated these qualities to
such incredible heights that he soared beyond
the limits of tragedy, and crossed that invisible
line into hilarious comedy."

"For years, we sat in the movie theaters and
screamed with laughter as this well intentioned
man suffered horribly at the hands of wives,
sweethearts, policemen, criminals, landlords,
jealous suitors and creditors, but all of these
people combined didn't wound him nearly as

deeply as did his constant companion."

"Stan Laurel vexed Oliver and frustrated him and inflicted physical havoc upon him at every turn in the road. And yet, you always knew that when the last reel had flickered out, Babe and Stan would still be together. You see, as a man of honor, dignity and chivalry, Babe Hardy could only choose to suffer along with a difficult friendship rather than try to end it."

"Stan Laurel was the architect of the team's brilliance - but it was Babe who made the relationship between them plausible. He was the one who made it work." We all know that Hollywood has produced hundreds of extremely talented comedic actors, but is there anyone among them who'd have made you believe that he would have suffered along with Stan's companionship in one film after another? No, I think not. Only a gentleman like Babe Hardy could have made it seem convincing.

How many times have we heard Babe introduce Stan by saying "This is my friend, Mr. Laurel?" Many, many times. But if you think back for a moment, no one ever introduced Babe. Never.

So let's remedy that situation. Ladies and gentlemen, a toast - I'd like to introduce our very good friend, - Mr. Oliver "Babe" Hardy.

My Goodness, Sir, Have You Ever Been to Louisa?

"Well, why then did you come back to Staunton?" the Commandant asked.

The Staunton Military Academy was an all-male military academy located in Staunton, Virginia for much of its 116-year history. Many notable American political and military leaders are graduates including:

- Winton M. Blount (1938), United States Postmaster General 1969-71
- John Dean (1957), White House Counsel 1970-73
- Barry Goldwater (1928), five-term United States Senator from Arizona (1953–65)
- Phil Ochs (1958), folk-protest singer
- A.J. Tim Rodenberg, Sheriff of Clermont County Ohio

Shortly after moving to Staunton, Virginia, in 1993, our elderly next-door neighbor, Eliza Christian, came over to welcome us to the Shenandoah Valley. Eliza told the following story about a cadet and the very small town of Louisa, Virginia:

One day a cadet ran away from the Staunton Military Institute. The commander decided there would be no manhunt for the young man.

A few days later the wayward youth returned to Staunton. The commander called him to his office for a debriefing.

"Where did you go, young man?" the General asked.

"I went to Louisa, sir," the boy answered.

"Well, why then did you come back to Staunton?" the Commandant asked.

"My goodness, sir," the young boy replied, "Have you ever been to Louisa?"

A Big League Story

"I couldn't tell what the cat did with the rabbit after that.

A couple of summers ago during a rain delay of a Cincinnati Reds baseball game, Joe Nuxhall began to tell a story about how one day he was sitting on his front porch and all of a sudden his house cat jumped out of the front door and started running quickly toward the front yard. Joe said he watched the cat dig and dig until he saw the cat pull a rabbit from the hole. "I couldn't tell what the cat did with the rabbit after that," Joe said.

"Joe, that's a big league story," Marty remarked.

Trip to New Orleans

Harold Reid, the bass singer for the Statler Brothers, lived just around the corner from us in Staunton, Virginia. Harold is the comic in the group, and is always good for a laugh or two.

Four or five years ago, near Mardi Gras time Staunton's newspaper, the Daily News-Leader, ran an article and a picture of a neighborhood Mardi Gras parade. The parade included a dog pulling a wagon. The dog had a pair of paper reindeer antlers on its head, as a baby-sat smiling in the wagon. There also was an old man playing a saxophone, along with a woman banging together two spoons. All in all, about six people participated in the parade.

The news reporter canvassed the neighborhood and interviewed several people. When he got to Harold, he asked him what he thought of the parade.

"Great, Harold said, it saved me a trip to New Orleans."

The Funeral Singer

"Son, that was very good, but you need to finish the last few stanzas with one breath."

The man said. "I really don't feel like singing, but I promised my wife that if anything ever happened to her I would sing her favorite hymn at a Requiem Mass."

With that, he stepped down from the altar before he began to sing at his wife's funeral.

He prefaced his singing with this story. "I first sang this song in this Catholic Church when I was seven years old. My mom believed I was a singer and somehow convinced the parish priest. She asked him if I could sing a solo Easter Sunday. I stood to the side of the altar, right over there, near the statue of the Virgin Mary, the man pointed. I was scared to death, but very determined to please my mom," he said.

When he finished the song, Ave Verum Corpus, his mother came over and said, "Son, that was very good, but you need to finish the last few stanzas with one breath."

"Oh, Mom, I don't think I can do that," he replied. "Those notes are too high for me and too difficult to sing," he protested.

"There are going to be times in your life, son, just like now with this song, that you are going to have to reach deep inside yourself and bring out the extra effort that will give you an advantage, to get you through," his mother said.

His mom was correct. There have been many times in his life that he has had to reach deep down inside himself to find that extra something, that grace his mother described to him so many years ago. "Today is another one of those times when I need the Gift from God, His grace and blessing to sing this tribute to my wife," the man said. "Today is the first time I have sung publicly in almost sixteen years. Please bear with me as I try to reach the high notes with one breath in the last stanza; as I attempt to honor and dedicate this most blessed hymn to the love of my life; as I say goodbye one last time," the singer said.

The man held the last note for 13 seconds and said goodbye to his wife.

The Trailways Bus

*Mom waved
good-bye to us
all as she headed
west to Redmond,
California, in the
heart of the Death
Valley Desert.*

In 1960, my mother, Ellen, decided she was going to visit my Uncle Robert and Aunt Mary in California.

Mom boarded a Trailways bus in Columbus, Ohio, and waved good-bye to us all as she headed west to Redmond, California, in the heart of the Death Valley Desert. Mom traveled alone and wound her way to Chicago, then to St. Louis, and on to Kansas City, traveling 1,459 miles west to Wichita to Los Angeles via Tucumcari and Albuquerque.

A few years earlier, in 1956, Continental Trailways took a bold step forward and began luxury bus service complete with an airline style hostess, reserved seats, pillows, magazines, music, use of an electric razor, lavatory equipped buses and food service. Trailways called it 5-Star Luxury Service and the first schedules ran on Continental Western Lines between New York and Los Angeles. Response was immediate and the schedules were running at near capacity from almost the beginning.

Of course, food service on board a bus was the main attraction. The menu included chilled fruit juices (tomato, orange and grapefruit), hot consommé, assorted sandwiches, donuts, cookies, and various beverages (coffee, hot chocolate, iced or hot tea, milk and soft drinks). The additional 5-Star service charge was only $2.00 and included all you cared to eat.

The grueling trip took 64 hours and the extra fare was $9.00, coast-to-coast which also included breakfast every morning off the bus!

Times have changed.

My Dad — A Man of Constant Good Humor

Twenty-six years after my father's death, I have grown to appreciate two things about him that have stuck with me more than anything else. During the 39 years of life we shared together, I never heard my dad utter one curse word nor ever take the name of our Lord in vain. Never.

Maybe it was because every night of his life he turned down his bed, knelt on his knees beside it, and said his evening prayers. My dad prayed every night of his life.

Danny Boy

I was proud that Greg cared enough about America to want to defend her freedom, as a father, I was worried for his welfare.

Danny Boy is adopted from an old Irish air. It is a love song, but not in the traditional boy-girl sense. It is, rather, a loving ballad from a caring father to his tender young son subsequent to the boy's departure to war. It is a timeless message, as pertinent now as it was centuries ago.

In 1991, Greg was attending the University of Rio Grande when I called his dorm to ask if he had heard the news of the United States armed forces invading Iraq. Greg said he and most of the boys in his dorm had stayed up all night watching the invasion on television. Greg also said many of the boys in his room wanted to enlist in the Army to help defend their country. I asked him if he was thinking about joining.

He said, "Yes, I would fight if matters worsened."

I had mixed emotions that day. I was proud that Greg cared enough about America to want to defend her freedom, but as a father, I was worried for his welfare.

With a sense of relief, I heard a report on the

radio that the Gulf War would be short and that casualties would be minimal for the United States.

Later that night, I thought of the words a worried father had written a couple of hundred years ago about his son who had gone off to war. The circumstances were different, as were the fresh young faces, but the worry of a father was still the same.

Oh Danny boy, the pipes, the pipes are calling.
From glen to glen, and down the mountainside.
The summer's gone, and all the flowers are dying,
'Tis you, 'tis you must go and I must bide.
But come ye back when summer's in the meadow,
Or when the valley's hushed and white with snow.
'Tis I'll be here in sunshine or in shadow,
Oh Danny boy, oh Danny boy, I love you so.

And if you come, when all the flowers are dying,
And I am dead, as dead I well may be.
You'll come and find the place where I am lying,
And kneel and say an "Ave" there for me.

Dwight Runs Away from Home

Mid-way through "Drop the Hankie" someone yelled out, "Dwight has run away from home!"

A few weeks ago, I was standing in McDonald's waiting in line when a former Port William First Grade classmate of mine, Dave Kline, walked over and tapped me on the opposite shoulder, hoping I would turn in the wrong direction. I didn't fall for that old trick, and turned the correct way right into Dave's smiling face.

It didn't take long before we were talking about our years in elementary school. We remembered how the music teacher, Ms. Daves, used to roll the piano from room to room for our sixty minutes of singing. "I loved to sing "The Happy Wanderer" every chance we got, which was about once a week," Dave said.

Dave told me how our Third-Grade teacher, Mrs. Ethel Gleason would take a student to the small, library and give the mischievous student a couple of whacks with the paddle. "Ace, Dave is the only person I know who calls me Ace, do you remember how Mrs. Gleason would them give you a hug after she gave the swats?" She would always say, "This hurt me more to do this than it did you."

"No, Dave. I don't know. I never received a paddling," I said to the great delight of my classmate. Having known me for almost sixty years, Dave just smiled.

"Do you remember Dwight Milburn's birthday party when we were in the First Grade?" Dave asked.

"I sure do," I replied. We played a lot of games and ate birthday cake." As we were chuckling, lo and behold, who would walk in but another classmate, Birthday boy, Dwight Milburn.

We told Dwight we had just been talking about him a few minutes earlier. We asked if he remembered his First Grade birthday party. "Yes. It sure was fun," Dwight said.

Dwight said he works at McDonald's now, and when he saw his two old friends talking, he wanted to stop by and join in the conversation. Dwight said he goes by his first name Darrell at work. "It is company policy," he said. He insisted we still call him Dwight, which was okay with us. We began to talk about his birthday party again. He said he remembers it well. "I do, too," I said. "Here is what I remember about the party."

When we were in the First Grade in 1955, we were invited to Dwight Milburn's 6th year birthday party on Hiney Road, outside Port William. Our entire class at Liberty Local School was invited – David Twine, Fred Ehlerding, Larry Runyan, David Kline, Linda Walls, Dee Siders, and Ruthie Dudley.

Ruthie and Dwight were, as we called them in those days, girlfriend – boyfriend.

Mid-way through "Drop the Hankie" someone yelled out,

"Dwight has run away from home!"

We all glanced toward Hiney Road and there was Dwight running toward Port William. Larry, Freddie, Dave, and I took off after him, caught him, and brought him back to the party. No more had we settled down, and then someone else yelled, "Dwight has run away again." Sure enough, Dwight once more was rounding the bend and picking up steam. Again, the group of boys caught up with Dwight, returned him home, and made him promise he wouldn't run away again.

Ruthie Dudley was beside herself because she and Dwight had had a tiff, and she thought she was the reason he decided to leave home. The next time Dwight took off running, the girls joined in, and we all caught Dwight again. Dwight ran off eight more times, and each time his guests had to go retrieve him. It became sort of a game itself.

When I arrived home after the party, my Mom asked if I had enjoyed myself. I told Mom that Dwight had run away from home eleven times, while we were there for his party, and that each time my friends and I chased him, caught him, and returned him home. Mom just looked out the window and smiled.

We did not know until much later that Dwight's parents had bought him a new pair of tennis shoes for his birthday. Whether the new shoes played a part in his absconding, we may never know for sure. Sometimes things are lost in the mists of time. But not in the minds of the boys of Port William.

Isn't Anything Free Anymore?

One neighbor brought us his generator and sump pump, for us to pump the water out of our basement.

Let me tell you a story. It's a story about people – and how people help each other.

On September 16, 2003, my wife, Brenda and I huddled around a bright, glowing candle as we listened to the strong winds of Hurricane Isabel knock down one tree after another in our neighborhood.

The next morning, we woke up and looked around to see what the wind had done to our home and those belonging to our neighbors. Tree limbs were laying all over our yard, and further down Taylor Street a huge tree had fallen across the electric wires knocking out the electricity of everyone on our block.

Our basement had almost 7 inches of water, which covered the bottom of our hot water heater and furnace. When we walked outside, we found most of our neighbors standing on the sidewalk talking with each other. They were asking what they could do to be of help. One man brought over his chain saw, and started cutting a tree that had fallen. Another started raking branches and putting them into bags. One neighbor brought us his generator and sump pump, for us to pump the water out of our basement.

On Monday, I woke up and realized that we still didn't have any hot water. I thought it was time to drive down to the YMCA and ask if I could take a hot shower.

"You sure can, but it will cost you two dollars," the nice woman said.

"I guess nothing is free anymore," I said as I handed her the money.

There is a song that says that the best things in life are free, and certainly, when looking at a sunset or a sunrise, we know that is true. After spending three days helping others without any expectation of being paid, I was a little disappointed with the lack of charity at the YMCA, which by the way, stands for the Young Men's Christian Association. Nevertheless, God works in mysterious ways, and having to pay the two dollars for the shower motivated me to think. Some things in this world need to be free.

Finally, on Saturday evening our electricity came back on. We were all tired but happy that we had the opportunity to help each other - just because we all needed help.

As we woke up Sunday morning, we realized we were going to have to take cold showers because we didn't have gas to warm our water. Then, after we stopped shivering and shaking, we went to church and thanked God for sparing us greater damage and asked Him to help those in greater need, and to give them the strength to see their way through this difficult time.

And one more thing, I learned that there are happy endings, too. As I was leaving the Y after my shower, the woman at the counter handed the two dollars back to me.

"Some things in life should be free," she said with a smile.

Letterman

Frank Sinatra once said, "There was no finer place on earth than New York City in the 1940's and 50's."

David Letterman once told actor Chris Elliott "that he suspected Elliott was the illegitimate product of an ill-considered wager that somehow had gone terribly wrong."

With those words in mind and after a brief discussion, my son, Greg, and I rented a new Camry and headed off to New York, New York (the city so nice they named it twice), for no reason other than to catch a taping of The Late Show with David Letterman. After settling into the Hampton Inn across the street from the Newark Airport, we raced through the Holland Tunnel to 1697 Broadway, the home of the Late Show with David Letterman and the Ed Sullivan Theatre. After speaking to CBS page, Erin, outside the theatre doors, we took our place in the line-up that had formed along Broadway. There we chatted with a variety of people who, like us, were there just for the experience. While we waited, we went around the corner to "The Hello Deli" to buy some lunch; and, of course, to meet Rupert Jee, one of Dave's neighborhood pals. Rupert, an unassuming man, was hard at work behind the cash register taking orders. "The Hello Deli" is, as you might predict by the camera shots of Rupert on the Letterman Show, quite small. T-Shirts with Rupert's face on 'em next to the cash register had the worn look of a product nobody wanted to buy. Greg and I ordered two simple sandwiches - a Chicken Salad Sandwich and a Smoked Turkey Breast Sandwich. Nothing too exciting, but the experience was great!

Greg and I were two typical tourists that knew no visit to New York City would be complete without a picture taken with Mujibur Rahman and Sirajul Islam, two more of Letterman's "characters". Greg walked into their souvenir shop, and as he introduced himself, he asked if he might have his picture snapped with them. Mujibur and Sirajul were most gracious, and I took several pictures of the trio collectively and individually.

There is no other place on earth like New York City, particularly when the sun goes down. As Greg and I milled around the CBS Studio, it became obvious there weren't going to be any extra tickets for that evening's show. At that point, we decided to take advantage of our time and turn our journey into an adventure. We scurried to the back of the Sullivan Theater, just in time to see Linda Ronstadt and Samuel L. Jackson, among other celebrities, enter the stage door. Biff Henderson opened the door wide and welcomed both stars enthusiastically, winking at Greg and me before he shut the door.

The longer Greg and I stood around the back door, the more we noticed the changing of the faces of those around us. The sun had set, and "street people", those who sleep all day and stay out all night, were slowly replacing many of the tourists who earlier had been by our side.

Our trip to New York was one both Greg and I will always remember. I had always wanted to see a tenement building in New York, and we were able to see several buildings that looked like they had been the location for the movie, "Singing in the Rain". I had also always wanted to eat in a New York deli, one like Art Carney and Jackie Gleason used to frequent in the "Honeymooners", and Rupert Jee was able to satisfy that desire.

Frank Sinatra once said, "There was no finer place on earth than New York City in the 1940's and 50's." Greg and I like to think we caught a little bit of that charm on our trip to Manhattan, even if it was fifty years later.

Twenty-seven Cents

"I quit." I said. "Anyone who would get mad over an honest mistake like mixing corn and green beans is too petty for me.

Some time ago, I found an old official-looking document from the Social Security Administration. The document included a listing of my taxed Social Security Earnings from 1966 to 2004. I quickly scanned the pages and discovered that I had earned a total of 27 cents in 1966. Piquing my attention, I decided the matter deserved further contemplation, so I sat back in my chair and let my mind drift back to that fateful day in 1966.

One Sunday afternoon I was sitting at home when it occurred to me that I would need extra spending money for the upcoming high school prom and dance.

I quickly scanned the Wilmington News-Journal, and saw an ad for a short order cook at a local restaurant.

I drove my dad's Ford to the local eatery and advised the owner I was answering the ad for the short order cook position advertised in the newspaper. The owner immediately had me fill out the proper paperwork including a Social

Security form; and then he took me to the kitchen. He quickly introduced me to the cook who looked and acted like Mel in the old television show Alice. The cook immediately handed me a hamburger flipper, told me to cook three hamburgers, and to add cheese to one of them. I thought this was going to be great, as I frequently cooked hamburgers for our family dinners. A few minutes after I finished handing the hamburger plate to the server, the owner came running over and shouted for me to quit "mashing the hamburgers so thin." I thought that was a reasonable request, as there wasn't much meat in the hamburger to begin with. Then, the owner once again entered the kitchen and criticized my baked beans and French fries. Since I was a new employee and eager to learn, I overlooked his sarcasm and consternation and continued to strain the green beans and corn. Within a few minutes, the owner returned to the kitchen angry and red-faced.

"Who mixed the green beans and corn together?" he demanded.

"I must have put the two vegetables a little too close together," I responded. "I didn't think any harm was done."

"Then you must not know very much," he retorted in the rudest of terms. Counting the insult as his last, I immediately bid the owner and the cook adieu and headed out the back door.

"Where are you going?" they growled.

"I quit." I said. "Anyone who would get mad over an honest mistake like mixing corn and green beans is too petty for me. That type of attitude does not motivate me. Please send me my check."

Three days later, I opened an envelope from the restaurant that contained a check for 27 cents. I grinned to myself and shook my head quietly.

Thanks to the United States Government, I have a permanent record of the 27 cents I earned, as well as a lesson learned. Over the years, I have learned to tolerate many things in this world, but rudeness is not one of them.

Christmas Legends

Perry Como and Bing Crosby were synonymous with carols and Christmas. Can you imagine being them, and walking in a mall and hearing your singing of Christmas carols piped throughout the stores?

Perry Como was performing a Christmas tour in a Midwestern town some years ago. After the show, much to the delight of surprised guests, Perry and his pianist made some music together in the lobby of the local hotel where they were staying. It is hard to imagine some of the current crop of singers standing around a piano singing Christmas Carols with total strangers, just because it was Christmas.

Fellow singer, Rosemary Clooney, said her most beautiful Christmas memory was the Christmas of 1955. She was delighted when Bing Crosby and his four sons sang carols outside the homes along Roxbury Drive in Beverly Hills, where she lived at the time. The famous carolers stood on Rosemary's porch and sang several songs in harmony, and then moved on down the street to entertain more neighbors.

Lowell Alexander of Bloomington, Picker Extraordinaire

Lowell ambled toward his car and waved one last time as he headed his big Nash Rambler up Gallimore Road.

This is one those stories that has faded with time, but a story, nevertheless, with many different perspectives. I'm sure each remembrance of the occasion is different as my sister, Rita, the birthday honoree; my mother, Ellen, the birthday party planner; and I, an eight-year-old brother, all came together one summer night in Port William.

It is my recollection the grand event took place on Rita's birthday or about July 14, 1955 or 1956; or perhaps it was Rita's graduation party from Port William High School that prompted the party. All I can remember is that Rita had invited all of her high school friends: Janet Twine, Mary Jo Shadley, Rosie Waldren, Myrna Gilliam, Donna King, and Ann Reno to a party one evening at our home in Port William, Ohio. My mother had hired Lowell Alexander, a resident of nearby Bloomington and one of the biggest entertainers in our area at the time, to sing and play his guitar at the party. I remember the unease of the young girls as he pulled his guitar out of the case and began to tune it. Mr. Alexander weighed about 350 pounds and filled-up the entire side of our old couch when he sat down in the front room, which was known as the "good room". He told a few jokes that met with a couple of nervous giggles and some stifled laughter, but essentially the girls were not warming-up to his old-fashioned showmanship style. Then all at once, Lowell broke into a nice soft ballad, and the girls began to soften. His clean tenor began to soar, along with his excellent picking of the guitar, and soon the girls were getting into the mood. They began to request one song after another, and he sang for about three hours until his repertoire was empty, as was his stomach.

"Thank you for inviting me, Mrs. Haley," I remember Mr. Alexander saying, "and Rita, have a happy birthday, happy graduation, or whatever it may be, and invite me back again."

"There goes a man who might be as big as Mac Wiseman someday," I remember thinking as Lowell ambled toward his car and waved one last time as he headed his big Nash Rambler up Gallimore Road back toward Bloomington.

Dad's Favorites

Another favorite activity of my Dad was listening to Waite Hoyt describe the play-by-play of the Cincinnati Reds.

My Dad, Robert Haley, always enjoyed watching talented comedic stars and comedy/entertainment shows. His favorites were Jack Benny and Rochester, Milton Berle, Red Skelton, Edgar Bergen and his wooden dummies, Charlie McCarthy and Mortimer Snerd.

Saturday evenings were a special time for our family, as an early television radio show sponsored by Purina Dog Chow featured the country singer, Eddy Arnold, one of Dad's favorite singers. He never ever missed a show.

Another one of my Dad's favorites was the television show called "Your Hit Parade". Although our family didn't have much money, we didn't care a bit. We enjoyed those special times together listening to the different shows.

Some of our fondest memories of my older brothers, Jim and Jack, and sister, Rita, were of those times when Dad took the family to the Murphy Theatre to see the "The Babe Ruth Story", featuring William Bendix as Babe Ruth.

My Dad was a connoisseur of the big screen. As careful as he was with his purse strings, Dad relaxed them whenever he had an opportunity to take our family to see a show. As I recall, we visited either the indoor Murphy Theatre or the Wilmington Drive-In almost once a week, so we were regulars. According to my brothers and sister, our mother, Ellen, loved to go the Murphy Theatre on Tuesday nights to see Wilmington native Kroger Babb's "The Best is Yet to Come".

Another favorite activity of my Dad was on hot summer nights sitting in our porch swing in our hometown of Port William, Ohio, listening to Waite Hoyt describe the play-by-play of the Cincinnati Reds ballgames. We could always look across the street and see "Inky" Ary, who was blind, doing the same thing. After the games, my Dad liked to relax with a good cigar, usually a "King Edward", and listen to radio channel WHIO, a Dayton station that played beautiful music 24 hours a day.

My dad loved baseball. He coached the Port William Tri-County baseball team, which included my brothers Jim and Jack as members, and my Uncle Patsy as the assistant coach.

Many times throughout each summer, Dad would load up our entire family in our 1937 Model A Ford and head for a Red's afternoon game at Crosley Field in Cincinnati.

Then there was Old River. Old River was a beautiful family park located about 40 miles away from our home in Dayton, Ohio. It was owned by my Dad's employer, National Cash Register, fondly referred to by many as (NCR) and by our family as simply, "The Cash". Old River was also a favorite of my Dad's, and a special place for all of our family. We watched a lot of baseball on those summer nights, long gone by.

A Quick Trip to the Big Apple

*They told Rita
that their mother
had moved to
New York City
and wouldn't be
coming back.*

According to my brother, Jack, the year was either 1944 or 1945, and my sister, Rita, was about six years old. Our family was living on Main Street in Port William, Ohio, next to Sander's Market. One afternoon our Mother had walked next door to the grocery store and unbeknownst to us, Rita had been looking for her. Suddenly, Rita appeared before my brothers, Jim, and Jack franticly asking them about Mom's whereabouts. Being typical ornery brothers and loving to tease their sister, they told Rita that their mother had moved to New York City and wouldn't be coming back. Rita went to pieces.

When Mom returned home and heard Rita crying, she asked Jim and Jack, "What is wrong with Rita Ann?" Although knowing they were doomed, they confessed to Mom what they had said to their sister to upset her. Mom was a believer in swift and direct punishment, so immediately; she made Jim and Jack sit on a chair. They were none too happy at that point, but knew they had it coming.

Almost sixty years have passed since that time, and subscribing to the theory that "confession is good for the soul," Jim and Jack agreed to offer our most humble apologies to their dear sister, Rita. When our deepest regrets were conveyed to Rita through their younger brother, Pat, about the long ago incident, her only response was, "Yeah, I bet they're sorry!"

Port William
Bank Robbery

Port William, like most small towns, have their share of laugher and heartbreak along with stories of adventure that are often passed down from generation to generation. The armed robbery of the Port William Bank is one such story.

On January 10, 1940, the Wilmington News Journal headline told the people of Clinton County: 'Bank Bandit Blown to Bits by Blast.' As is true in most stories, there was a human being behind the headlines and captions.

According to accounts of my parents, and many of the local old-timers who handed the tale down through the years, Forrest Miller was well-known and well-liked within the farming community of Sabina. Although a bit shy and somewhat of a loner (the boy who lived and walked alone, some called him), Forrest nevertheless was popular. He was regarded as a good boy to all who knew him. In 1933, however, something went terribly wrong in Forrest's life. He was convicted of burglary and sent to the Mansfield Reformatory. Upon his release, Forrest moved to Reesville and tried his hand at farming. He was young and restless, and the satisfaction other farmers achieved from their work was missing for Forrest. He did odd jobs around Sabina, but spent most of his days idling away the time.

In 1935, Forrest turned twenty years of age. He was still restless and had too much time on his hands. One night he decided to break into a business on the west side of Sabina. In those years, justice was swift. He was apprehended, convicted and this time sent to the Ohio Penitentiary in Columbus, Ohio. The four years he spent at the Spring Street prison were long and hard. After his release, Forrest was anxious to resume a normal life and swore off, for the last time, a life of crime.

At first things went well for him. He moved to Bowersville into his own home. Although it was modest, called a shack by some, it was his home. He did odd jobs around town, and even returned to the farm he loved. He met a young woman and fell in love. The years in prison were not kind to Forrest. He had been a private person before, but afterward he had a hardness about him that betrayed his years. He was twenty-five years old, and in love with a nice young woman. For a time, the couple was happy. Forrest, however, found it hard to shake-off his years behind bars. Many of his old friends had shunned him since his release from prison, and it became apparent to the woman that he was seldom free from the demons that were resident within him. She left Forrest. Many men in like circumstances might have said they were unlucky in love and moved on. That is what Forrest Miller planned to do, but Forrest didn't make much money as a farmer's helper. He needed more cash in order to travel to Arizona or New Mexico, where he planned to start a new life for himself.

It had snowed for several days and there was still substantial snow accumulation on the ground when Forrest, dressed in a shabby overcoat and a hunter's cap, entered the front door of the Port William Bank. He had been in the bank the day before, so bank cashier, Howard Hiatt, didn't think much about it when Forrest walked through the front door. That time it was different. Forrest walked over to Mr. Hiatt and demanded money. Forrest handed him a note that said, 'Put the money in this bag or I'll blow your brains out.' At that point, Forrest pulled out a small bottle of liquid and loudly announced that he had a bottle of nitroglycerin in his hand. One of the tellers had initially thought the man was playing a joke, because the liquid in the bottle looked like plain drinking water. However, the look in Forrest's eyes made the two men decide to err on the side of caution. Doing just as the robber had requested they handed him $324.21 - a fair amount of money during the Depression era.

Forrest quickly ran from the bank; as Assistant Bank Cashier, Robert Shrack, sounded a silent alarm that had been wired to G.W. Stephens and Sons Hardware store next door to the bank. Just as quickly, a posse formed that included Mayor Louis Haines, Paul Stryker, Roy Beal, and Robert Shrack. G. W. (Bill) Stephen's grabbed a shotgun from the hardware's gun case and fired two blasts in the rear window of the fleeing automobile.

My parents, Bob and Ellen Haley, lived next door to the bank. My oldest brother, Jim, recalled many years later that he was four years-old at the time, and remembers the men running down the sidewalk in front of the bank, excitedly shouting at the man to stop.

The posse had quickly begun a hot pursuit after the local citizens spotted a white Chevrolet speeding through the center of town heading north on snow-covered Garber Road (now known as Gallimore Road).

Another carload of Port William men soon joined the chase, and as the two cars sped north, one behind the other, the men were gaining on the wayward bandit. Suddenly, they reached the two hairpin curves located on the road, near where the Interstate 71 overpass is located today. The robber successfully navigated the first dangerous curve, but the second one proved too brutal for his old Chevy. Losing control, the robbers' car rolled over several times before it landed on its top in the freshly-picked cornfield.

"We have him now!" the men shouted, as they leaped from their car determined to bring the man to justice. With that, a terrific explosion occurred with the overturned vehicle that old-timers say shook the windows clear to Jamestown, about ten miles away. The shaken men ducked and quickly ran back to their cars. Looking back at the site of the explosion, there was no doubt the bank robber had met justice.

The Clinton County Sheriff and Coroner were called and Forrest's body was removed from the badly damaged automobile and taken to Littleton's Funeral Home in Sabina. He was later interred in the Sabina Cemetery.

It was not long ago that I was talking with Earl and Don Stryker, sons of Paul, one of the posse members, about the Port William Bank robbery that had occurred more than seventy years ago.

"A few weeks after the robbery, our dad received an envelope from the Port William Bank in the mail," said Earl. "Inside was a dollar bill encased in a paper money holder along with a note thanking him for pursuing the bank robber. Dad kept that dollar for the rest of his life. It represented more than money to him," Don said. It was the memory of a town that cared for each other and about the young 'boy who lived and walked alone.'

The Next Voice You Hear

Years ago, in Cincinnati, there was a television show called the Schoenling All Night Theater, which ran from 1:30 am to 6:00 am on Sunday mornings. Some will remember the host, Bob Shreve, who was full of shenanigans and tomfoolery.

The movie this particular morning was The Next Voice You Hear, starring James Whitmore and Nancy Davis (later known as Mrs. Ronald Reagan). They played a typical all-American post-war couple.

One day they heard a voice on the radio: "This is God talking. I'm going to be with you for the next few days."

The movie had opened with a picture of the streets of Los Angeles, crowded with people in cars and buses busily rushing from intersection to intersection, honking their horns, and swerving to miss pedestrians. The freeways were at a standstill as drivers sat in their cars, aggravated as their cars sat bumper-to-bumper.

The camera then turned its attention to the

next scene; office workers were running from place to place, not taking the time to be civil to each other. At the end of the day, James Whitmore jumped into his car, honked at everyone in sight, spewed a few curse words, and sped home. He shook his fists at other drivers who pulled out from their driveways or intersections almost causing collisions.

When Whitmore arrived home, he immediately brushed off his young son. The little boy had run up to his dad's car full of excitement, in anticipation of his dad's arrival home from work. Whitmore's rejection caused the child to cry, then to run off to his bedroom with a pitiful expression on his face. Next, Whitmore berated his wife when she welcomed him home. He brushed her off when she tried to give him a kiss. This behavior continued all evening, until Whitmore finally settled down and turned on the radio to listen to his favorite program.

As Whitmore listened to the radio, he occasionally let out a loud laugh when his favorite entertainer said something amusing. His wary family sat near him, careful not to say or do anything that would set Whitmore off. The scene began to change when Whitmore heard a strange voice speaking on the radio. He was unable to make out the voice, but thought it was part of the program. Later, the voice returned even louder and announced, "This is God speaking." At first, Whitmore was amused and disbelieving. As the voice continued addressing the hurried pace of the world and the number of unbelievers, Whitmore and his family became a bit more concerned. Then the voice said he would be on the radio every night for the next 7 evenings.

Whitmore dismissed the voice as a stunt, and reassured his wife and son who appeared to be frightened.

The traffic scene the following morning, though less hurried, contained fast and reckless driving. When Whitmore arrived at his office, a man at the water cooler asked him if he had heard the voice on the radio the previous night. Whitmore laughed, saying he thought it was an amazing, clever stunt for the radio show to fool its audience. The man told Whitmore he had heard on the radio that reports had come from all over the world, and that the voice had been heard in every country, at precisely the same time. The man said each broadcast had been in the native tongue. At once, Whitmore's smile vanished, and a look of apprehension replaced his appearance of amusement.

He was anxious to leave work to get home. He couldn't wait to turn on the radio that night and to see if the voice came on the air again. When Whitmore arrived home, his demeanor had softened considerably, and he spent more time than usual with his wife and his son that evening.

The voice indeed returned on the radio at exactly 8:00 p.m. Once more, the voice told the audience He was God, and he was disappointed with the people on earth. He told the audience He expected to see a change in the behavior of His "children" or there would be dire consequences.

The next morning we notice Whitmore stopping and talking with the milkman. Although he is still in hurry, he was becoming more patient started to sink in. The traffic jams appeared less demanding and the personalities of the drivers were more pleasant. The atmosphere at his office was much less stressful. People had begun taking time to talk with each other. The scenes continued to improve day by day, as God finally convinced the people His voice was not a radio stunt. At the end of seven days, everyone was living in perfect harmony.

The beauty of this short, sweet movie lay in its telling of the Golden Rule - "Do unto others as you would have them do unto you." The movie struck a chord with the public, because people secretly yearn for reassurance there is more to life than work and aggravation. We want to know that God is watching over us and that He will reward us for our good deeds. We all yearn for love; and even in our current reckless, cynical culture, we need to know there is something better for those who believe."

Our Next Election is Fast Approaching.

We were reminded why we should stand for America.

Everywhere we turn the news media is ablaze with the latest story of the candidates who question each other's statements, facts and honesty.

Remember the time when a candidate stood-up and simply said what was on his mind and in his heart? Now, they make great effort to belittle, rebuke, blame and demean the other side. They establish 'truth squads' to follow candidates around with video cameras and tape recorders hoping for a gaffe that will find its way onto the national news or at the very least, YouTube. The goal is to discredit their opponent, to make them look like a boob.

Far too many partisans subscribe to the Vince Lombardi philosophy that "winning isn't everything, it's the only thing." Some of us at the grass roots level sense that our way of life is being threatened, and winning an election isn't the only thing. It is time that 'Winning for America' becomes the only thing.

I know exactly what I want in this election. I

want a candidate who puts politics aside and does what is best for America. I want someone who sticks to his heartfelt beliefs. I want someone who believes today what he said he believed yesterday. I want someone who puts our country and the working people of this country first. I want someone who speaks from his heart and with conviction.

This past Tuesday, a day with brilliant blue skies and pleasant temperatures in downtown Wilmington, we came together once more to remember the 11th anniversary of the horrific terrorist attack against our country. We remembered how our nation was horror-struck and how we joined together and set aside partisan politics for a few weeks. We didn't criticize each other, we didn't twist the facts of our leaders. We stood united as a country. At least for awhile. We were all Americans, frightened of the unknown, but filled with resolve to bring those responsible to justice. We stood together. We wrapped ourselves in our flag, and as we grieved we discovered a strength we had not seen for far too many years.

We were reminded why we should stand for America. On September 11, 2001, we felt America with every fiber of our being. We grew to love her more with every tear that we shed on that terrible day in New York, Arlington, Virginia and Johnstown, Pennsylvania.

Leaders have always stood for their countries.

In 1939, during parliamentary debate on the coming war in

Europe, Prime Minister Neville Chamberlain finished another of his hopeful, frightened speeches about making peace with Hitler. A member of Parliament, Arthur Greenwood, rose to speak in opposition. As he did, the voice of a colleague pierced the chamber. "Speak for England, Arthur!" he called. The chamber erupted.

I want someone to speak for America.

Soldiers Returning

Let me get those, the old man said, weeping, as he stooped over to pick up the duffel bags of his 35-year old son

There are still towns with old Southern antebellum homes, live oak trees covered in moss, and sandy lanes like those that led us to the front porch of Tara in Gone With the Wind. Staunton, Virginia, is one such town.

Nicknamed the 'Queen City of the Shenandoah,' Staunton is rich in natural beauty, remarkable charm and renowned for its military traditions. Staunton is an old town, dating back to 1742 when her sons left the village to battle Indians. Colonel George Washington commanded a group of fellow Virginians during the French and Indian Wars. Generals Robert E. Lee and Thomas Jonathan 'Stonewall' Jackson fought up and down the Shenandoah Valley during the Civil War. They presently rest just a few miles down the road in Lexington, Virginia.

The Thomas D. Howie Memorial Armory, home to the 116th Brigade, 29th Infantry Division whose history predates our Declaration of Independence, sits high on a hilltop inside Staunton's beautiful Gypsy Hill Park. In the

Civil War, this unit served under Confederate Gen. Thomas J. "Stonewall" Jackson. It is the Stonewall Brigade.

There was a time, June 6, 1944, when the Stonewall Brigade, again made history. Staunton teachers, factory workers, farmers and bankers were the first Americans to land on the sandy beaches of Normandy during the early morning drizzle and fog on that long and terrifying day. Although they seized Omaha Beach, scores of young men from Staunton still lie in the American Cemetery in the tiny village of St. Laurent, France. Lieutenant Thomas Howie, the armory's namesake, died from shrapnel as he stood and fought with the Stonewall Brigade.

A few years ago, the Stonewall Brigade was returning from a tour of duty in Baghdad after a year of heavy fighting. Wanting to pay our respects, a neighbor and I made our way to the park. Quietly arriving at the armory, we stood on a hill away from the families and the returning soldiers. The dark sky offered rain while a strong, chilly wind swept through the crowd.

The cheer started as an undertone growing into a loud shout as a bevy of buses roared up the narrow side of the road. We could see the soldiers smiling and waving through the bus windows at the hundreds of waiting family members. Suddenly, the bus doors opened. Wives, husbands, mothers, fathers and children rushed the doors of the buses, hoping to see a glimpse of their loved ones and to know they were safely home.

We saw a man of about seventy years of age walk toward his son. They embraced long and hard. "Let me get those," the old man said weeping as he stooped over to pick-up the duffel bags of his thirty-five-year-old son.

"I can get them, Dad," the young man said smiling.

We all understood. That is just what fathers do. His elderly mother stood nearby, quietly crying and wiping away tears, with a look of relief only a mother can feel.

We stood off to the side of the stairs, out of the way. There were reporters. There were politicians and men running for office. There was clamor and confusion.

Then we saw him. We saw the old man standing on the top step. He looked to be 80-years-old. He was a military man. He stood ramrod straight and perfectly still, even in the howling wind.

As the young soldiers passed, they told their families about the hot sands of Bagdad. "He knows about sand, too," my neighbor whispered to me as he nodded toward the old man. "He wore the uniform of the Stonewall Brigade once. He fought his way across the sand at Omaha Beach."

We turned around just in time to see a young officer walking up the steps. He was weighted down, and walking rapidly through the crowd, eager to get home.

"Welcome home, and thank you," the old man said, reaching for his hand.

"Thanks," the young Captain responded a bit impatiently as he walked past the old soldier.

Just then, I heard one of the reporters say, "He's a D-Day veteran."

Suddenly, the young officer stopped, turned around, and took a step back. "Thank you," he said firmly grasping the old veteran's hand again. "Thank you, Sir."

As we left the armory, the strong wind that blew through the nearby Blue Ridge Mountains for the last couple of days lowered its breath, and the community lowered their eyes in thankful prayer. Once again, the great and fabled Stonewall Brigade had come home. Our prayer is they never leave again.

This Memorial Day let us remember and thank the many who have defended our freedom and served our nation.

A 'Melodee' to Remember

A man threw a cheeseburger at her-with tartar sauce on it-and said she rubbed it on his windshield.

The other evening, my wife, Brenda and I were sitting at the kitchen table reconciling our checking account when we found a curious receipt from Wilmington Frisch's restaurant. The receipt had the name 'Big Boy-Melodee' printed on it.

"Do you remember the Mel-O-Dee Restaurant?" Brenda asked with a bit of bemusement, knowing this type of question would generate a story.

"Oh, yes," I said as a smile began to spread across my face as my mind shifted back to the early days of both the Mel-O-Dee and the original Frisch's restaurant.

According to the old timers, Frisch's Big Boy first came to town with a pledge to 'Keep a smile on your face and your stomach full'. It was originally located on West Main Street just west of Bill Marine's Ford.

It was a true 'drive-in' restaurant with carhops dressed in crisp-looking uniforms. It definitely had a Happy Days and American Graffiti look about it.

The red-and-white dining room was small, complete with ten or so bar stools at the counter, a few booths and a couple tables. Family friend, Billy Hughes, of Port William was a cook at the time. He wore a white paper hat, positioned a bit off-center, with Frisch's name emblazoned on the side.

Kathy Smith remembers delivering orders to the cars when the other waitress was on break. On Friday and Saturday nights, they had two carhops and two waitresses.

The old Frisch's was a humming place. Becky Thumma recalls stopping there after play practice. Mary Lou and David Sprowl were courting around that time, but would take time to stop and enjoy a piece of strawberry pie while watching kids cruise the parking lot. Judy Schnatz and Sheryl Sollars remember the restaurant as a regular stop for Kingman's winning basketball team and cheerleaders.

Known not only for classic food, Frisch's was also known for music and contests. Pam Woods Hatcher, a former classmate, remembers entering a Hula-Hoop contest there.

"We were told a prize would be given to the person who could keep the Hula-Hoop spinning around our body for the longest period of time," Pam said warming to the subject. "I actually won second place. I could have kept 'hooping', but another girl faked me out pretending her Hula-Hoop was dropping to the ground. I dropped mine, and before I knew it, the girl wiggled hers back-up and someone declared her the winner!" "I think the adults were glad the contest was over. It lasted more than four hours," Pam remembered.

It left an indelible mark on her memory. "Just last summer," she said proudly, "I introduced the Hula Hoop to my granddaughter. Guess it's like riding a bicycle …."

On the other side of town sat the Mel-O-Dee Restaurant. A family restaurant, the Mel-O-Dee was similar in design to Frisch's, but lacked the signature Frisch's food. In the late 50's or early 60's, Frisch's moved to the Mel-O-Dee location and converted it to the present day restaurant.

Some people partook for the food, and some went for the adventure. Dave Moore used to order Marshmallow Cokes. "It was a concoction like no other. They would put soft marshmallows on the top of a glass of Coke, completely sealing the glass," Dave laughingly said. "A few shakes and the gas had nowhere to go but straight-up. Sweet explosion!"

There was another reason to go to the new Frisch's. If you were a teenager, which I was at the time, you went to cruise…and boy did we cruise.

Many evenings around six o'clock, I'd call the Doak residence on Accommodation Road. "Mrs. Doak is Ralph there?" I would ask.

"No, he's down at the old Conlin place," Margaret Doak would respond with a slight chuckle. "Would you like for me to ask him to call you?"

"Yes, that'd be fine. We're going to ride around town tonight," was the usual conversation.

Several times a week, after we had completed our homework,

Ralph and I would meet-up with friends, John Reynolds and Dan Dehan and head for Frisch's for a night of cruising.

It never failed. We'd find many of our classmates there as well, especially on the weekends. Penny Snyder, Marcia Ames and others would stroll by, and we'd call them over to the car and talk for hours.

Some of our friends worked there, too. Vickie Kendall served as a carhop. She recounted leaving the job because a man threw a cheeseburger at her - with tartar sauce on it - and said she rubbed it on his windshield. "I'd do it again," she said with a laugh. "For a variety of reasons."

It was a different time, yes. Still today, when we circle Frisch's, I can almost see the friendly carhop ready to serve-up food, and expect old friends to cruise-by. Many things have changed, but there was a time if you hadn't ridden around Frisch's on a Friday night, on to the Shopping Center, and then to the west side of town at least ten times, you weren't ready to go home yet.

Just ask my friends.

The Cincinnati Reds: Marge, Joe and the Smoking Shoes

My thoughts quickly drifted to baseball, which, in a sense, is in America's blood.

Monday evening was one of those rare nights when time moved slowly, and life was easy. The shadows had begun to steal across the lawn, lingering on my hammock as I stretched back just in time to hear the music announce that the Reds were on the radio.

My thoughts quickly drifted to baseball, which in a sense, is in America's blood. We play it. We watch it. We listen to it.

Several years ago, I had the good fortune to accept a unique position with Burns Security to oversee security for the Cincinnati Reds. As I put together the security team, I called on several friends from Wilmington to join us. Good friend and long-time Wilmington educator, Tim Martin, was one of those. Still today, we often talk of the days when he worked down on the playing field. According to Tim, it was a vantage point that made his summer "the stuff that dreams are made of."

Marge Schott was the owner of the Reds during our time with the team. She had learned that I was from Wilmington and one evening she approached saying, "I was on Rombach Avenue this morning. They want me to invest in the Wal-Mart in Wilmington, but I haven't made up my mind. What do you think?" she questioned.

"Well, I'm no expert, but from what I understand they seem to be a very sound investment," I shouted as the elevator door slammed shut.

A few weeks later, she volunteered in passing that she declined the offer to invest in the local Wal-Mart.

Every September, on 'Fan Appreciation Night' the Reds gave away prizes to the fans. On this particular night, Marge, who wasn't always portrayed in the best light but was a character in the kindest way, had decided that she would give away a new Chevrolet from her Cincinnati car dealership. The plan was to draw a number from a large drum, and present the new car to the winner down on the field. In an impatient mood that evening, Marge waited only about five or six minutes before announcing she was going to draw another name. I cautiously mentioned to her that it might take fifteen minutes for the winner to make it down to the field.

"That is too bad!" she responded. "If they want this car bad enough they need to get down here quicker!" She ended-up drawing numbers three more times. I have often wondered how many cars Marge eventually gave away that night.

Of all the people and celebrities I met during my time with the Reds, one stood out from the others. He was a tall, gregarious man with a natural laugh that had brightened the radio broadcasts of the Reds for almost 40 years. Joe Nuxhall.

Late one night after a game with the Cubs, we were leaving the stadium, and suddenly heard loud laughing in the parking garage near the parking attendants' station. Joe Nuxhall stood in the midst of the stadium workers, drawing them in, as he told a story about the best practical joker in baseball.

According to the Joe, one summer night in Dodger Stadium a fellow who was a relentless practical joker had been relaxing in the clubhouse reading a book on electronics when he came up with an extraordinary idea.

"This guy was crouched in the dugout holding a remote control device he had just purchased. His intended target was the Dodger's first base coach, who spoke little to no English," Joe said warming up to his subject.

"He had rigged the coach's spikes before the game with a remote-controlled flaming device. At first, we saw a couple of puffs of smoke drifting up from the grass around the first base coach's box," Joe laughed. "Soon, thick white smoke was emitting from the coach's shoes, but the coach was so engrossed in the game that he didn't notice the commotion. All at once, there was a great flash, and then two more in rapid succession. At first, the coach thought his spikes had struck a rock causing a spark. Then he realized his shoes were on fire. He jumped up and down wildly, fanning the flames on his shoes, and then he tried to run into the outfield hoping the dew on the grass would quench the flames. The coach finally ripped-off his shoes off and threw them in the dirt."

"That was a beauty," I heard Joe tell the laughing men. "I gotta go. See you later."

Marty and the Cowboy do the Reds broadcast now, but never a time passes when I glance over at the radio that I don't think of Joe, and that one magical night when he stood surrounded by working men, telling a great story.

And on those slow, easy evenings when the sun, the shadows, and a warm summer breeze all come together at the right moment, I can still 'the Old Lefthander' every time the Reds are on the radio.

Wilbur Tucker — A Man Who Drank Deeply From the Cup of Life

Deputy Tucker, walked over to the bull, slit its throat and put his fingers in the bull's neck.

"Sheriff, a bull has escaped from the Wilmington Livestock and is running east on Route 22 and 3 toward Sabina," Dispatcher Paul Starkey said over my mobile police radio.

"I will head that direction," I said.

Several deputies responded in short order and the more the officers chased the bull, the more scared and dangerous it became. After almost 30 minutes of pursuit, a deputy radioed that he had spotted the bull at Laurel Oaks Vocational School campus. Just then, Captain Mike Cluxton and I saw the bull running at full speed in a large open space far away from the people and buildings on the campus.

"Can you drop the bull?" I asked Captain Cluxton.

"Sure, Sheriff," the Captain said as he squeezed the trigger of the .30-caliber carbine.

The bull immediately fell to its kneels, then onto the ground. A couple of seconds later, one of the strangest things I have ever seen in my many years of law enforcement occurred. Deputy Wilbur Tucker, an elderly deputy who transported prisoners for the Sheriff's Department, arrived and asked us how long the bull had been dead. Deputy Tucker, a former butcher for the Kroger Company, walked over to the bull, slit its throat and put his fingers in the bull's neck. Wilbur had the bull's blood on his fingers and slowly raised his hand to his mouth.

"He is a little salty from all of the running, but I think he is still fit to butcher," Wilbur said.

After recovering from my shock of watching a man taste bull's blood, I turned to Captain Cluxton and said, "Hook him, Miko."

Mr. Froggy Goes A Courtin'

Suddenly, a terrific scream emitted from the restroom, just before she bolted through the door!

My tenure with the Wilmington Police Department was an experience, with its share of humor and practical jokes. There was a plethora of jokesters within the department, but it seemed one officer worked extra hard to perfect his shenanigans, almost reaching an art form.

One hot, summer night, he was working the midnight shift. He pulled the cruiser down Fife Avenue near City Park pond. Suddenly, a jumbo bullfrog hopped onto the roadway in front of our cruiser. The officer stopped the car and picked up the bullfrog. For some unknown reason, he decided the bullfrog's best chances for survival rested in the women's bathroom, located on the second floor of the City Building. He waited until about 5:00 a.m., and then he quietly entered the ladies room, placed the bullfrog inside the commode, and quickly shut the lid.

The long-time police clerk was an elderly woman. The officer knew the clerk had a daily ritual of starting her workday with a trip to the ladies' room, which incidentally, was located just past the Municipal Courtroom.

The officer stood hidden at the end of the hall, quietly watching the clerk as she entered the ladies' room. Suddenly, a terrific scream emitted from the restroom, just before she bolted through the door, running down the public hallway past the Mayor's Office. The Mayor came out of his office laughing so hard he had tears in his eyes. Ladies from inside the Municipal Court, as well as, the City Clerk's Office came tearing down the hall expecting the worse. When they reached the much shaken police clerk, she was standing above the commode, watching a gigantic bullfrog swimming in the toilet. Just then we heard a soft voice retort, "I can't understand who would do such a thing!" the officer opined. "Maybe the frog crawled up through the plumbing." And with that it was time to go home.

The Rookie

Just then, Brenda felt an unfortunate kick of the gun in her right hand as she accidentally squeezed the trigger.

My wife, Brenda, was a member of the Rookies, a membership organization for female college students enrolled in the Law Enforcement program at Eastern Kentucky University. She was a sophomore at EKU, a newly declared Law Enforcement major, and a brand new member of the Rookies. According to Brenda, she was nineteen years of age and was very excited about going to the shooting range and firing a gun for the first time in her life.

As she made her way to the firing line, she suited-up in a bulletproof vest and earphones to keep the noise level down on the range. The firing range was a state-of- the-art underground facility, crowded with other male and female Law Enforcement students and full-time police officers.

The firing instructor had forewarned us that safety was of paramount importance and that he would not tolerate any "Barney Fifes" on the range.

"Use much caution and care because these .357

magnums you are using could put a 12" hole in a person," he said. My wife nodded and thought to herself how good she felt because of the level of confidence shown her by the instructors.

As the afternoon shooting practice drew to a close, she was full of excitement and pride for having done so well for her first time. Brenda was eagerly anticipating the scores being tabulated by the firing instructor. As she "dismounted" from the range and began taking off the earphones and vest, she checked the gun cylinder to make sure all six rounds had been used and that the chamber was empty. With that step complete, Brenda proceeded toward the instructor to return her firearm and to leave the range.

Just then, Brenda felt an unfortunate kick of the gun in her right hand as she accidentally squeezed the trigger, discharging a live round of ammunition, that unbeknownst to her, was still inside the gun cylinder. It was like an out-if-body experience! She couldn't believe what she had done. The explosion was deafening. As Brenda quickly scanned the room, she saw people diving for cover and hitting the floor.

The instructor was yelling, "Everybody down" as Brenda heard the ricocheting bullet buffering off the walls and floor of the firing range.

Once the ricocheting stopped, the red-faced instructor and ·a hoard of breathless officers and students ran over to Brenda questioning what the heck had happened.

"I thought I told you to be careful, "one of the instructors bellowed.

"I didn't think it was loaded," Brenda said.

Milton Hershey Made Chocolate and Men

Mr. Hershey gave each of us a choice. He would pay for our college or we could become master chocolate makers

He was standing in the back of the store, all alone and dressed all in white. A white paper hat, like those handed out to kids now at Steak N Shake or Dunkin Donuts, sat just off the center of his head. His white pants and shirt resembled those favored by bakers.

The man was about fifty-years old with a bright smile and an engaging personality. "Welcome, folks. Come in. What brings you to Gettysburg?" he asked.

"We were touring the area and saw your sign out front, advertising chocolate," we said. "We also saw you standing near the two large copper kettles stirring chocolate and couldn't resist the aroma," my wife, Brenda added.

"How long have you been making chocolate?" we asked.

"Since I was a young boy. I have been at it a few years now," the man laughed, handing us each a piece of fresh chocolate with an almond in the middle.

We introduced ourselves and told him we were from Ohio. "I have some friends in Ohio. They are Amish and live near Millersburg," he said. "My name is Will," he said shaking our hands.

The man said he was taking a break from stirring the chocolate, and pulled up a chair near the door to enjoy the fresh breeze. Brenda and I sat down on a couch as he poured us both a nice glass of cool water.

The man said he had lived in Gettysburg for five years. He said he lived with his wife and four sons in a converted store a couple of blocks down the street.

Pulling off his hat and wiping his forehead the man took a long drink of water. "I never knew my parents," he began. He said he was born in the Amish country near Lancaster, Pennsylvania in the late 1940's. "1947, to be exact," he laughed.

"I grew up in the Milton Hershey Orphanage in Hersey, Pennsylvania. It was called the Hershey Industrial School when I lived there," he said. "It is now the Milton Hershey School."

He said his mom and dad were killed in an auto accident when he was very young, and he had no other family. He said the criteria for the orphanage at the time was 'to be poor, healthy, male and between the ages of eight and eighteen years of age.' He laughed and said he qualified on all accounts.

Will said Mr. Hershey and his wife, Kitty, were wonderful people. They had died a few years before his birth, but he said the older boys told him they were just like parents to them. They cared about people, especially kids since they had no children of their own.

Will said there were rules at the school they had to follow. "Mr. Hershey expected us to learn about God and responsibility," he said. "He wanted us to receive a good education, and feel a sense of stability and security," Will continued.

"We had to make our own beds every morning, and each child had to learn a vocation," he said.

"The happiest years of his life were spent in the orphanage. We never heard of drugs, and very few kids got into serious trouble," Will said. "Most of my friends are now well-adjusted with wonderful families of their own. No one felt inferior because they knew they were loved and cared for by the kind people at the Hershey School," he added.

"When it was time to graduate from high school, I had a decision to make," Will stated. Mr. Hershey gave each of us a choice. He would pay for our college or we could learn to become master chocolate makers at the school and factory. Will said one of older boys who knew Mr. Hershey said the famed chocolate maker once said, "The thing that a poor boy needs is knowledge of a trade, a way to make his living. We will provide him with the groundwork."

Will said he chose to learn the trade of chocolate making. His said his life changed for the better when he made that decision. "They even gave me $100.00 when I left the orphanage. I am making much more now," he laughed.

With that, he walked back to the kettles and started to slowly stir the chocolate again. We said goodbye and resumed our journey.

"Will may have been poor at one time, but he seems to be one the richest men I have ever met," I said to Brenda.

"Yes. I now fully understand why they call Hershey, Pennsylvania "The Sweetest Place on Earth," she added.

The Week Jim Let His Hair Down in Music City

I was sitting at home in Sabina when the phone rang. It was my brother, Jim. "Dean and I are in Nashville. Dean is on the Bill Anderson Show, Fandango, and is winning big. Why don't you come down?" Jim asked.

"You know, I think I will," I replied.

With those words, I traveled to Nashville and met Jim and Dean at the Opryland Complex. Nashville is one of my favorite towns, and it didn't take much prodding for me to join in the festivities.

One of the first things I remember thinking was, that something was different with Jim. I don't believe I had ever seen him so "loose". He was in good spirits and I could tell he was really in his element. We had rooms at the motel across from Opryland, and we spent a great deal of time touring the city together.

We really enjoyed watching Dean compete on the television game show – he did quite well. Dean's knowledge was truly amazing. Bill Anderson was never able to throw him a curve.

Regardless of the topic, Dean stepped-up to either answer the question or sing the song.

One night after the show, the three of us decided to go downtown to "see the sights". Jim was hilarious. He wanted to visit the "Pink Pussycat", a notorious nightclub in Printer's Alley.

As we passed the nightclub, a young woman came out of the doorway and said, "You look like three guys looking for some fun."

"We sure are," Jim responded, and with that, we entered the bar.

There was loud country music playing and a couple of girls dancing near the bar. We drank a few, had a few laughs, and then were then on our way back to the motel.

The next day, Jim and I were sitting in the television studio where they taped Fandango. We were watching Bill Anderson's assistants pick members from the audience to be contestants on that day's show. A young woman sat down next to me. I thought to myself that she sure looked familiar. After a few minutes, it dawned on me that this was the same woman who had stated to Jim the night before "that we looked like we were looking for some fun." Jim was sitting two chairs away from me and the "No Talking" sign was on, making it difficult for me to get his attention. I kept coughing until Jim looked at me. I nodded my head at the woman, and mouthed the words "Printer's Alley". Jim could not make out what I was saying, and looked at the woman thinking I thought she was someone famous. I shook my head, and mouthed the words, "looking for a good time". With that, Jim's eyes widened.

We laughed at the same time and one of Bill's assistants came running over and said, "Shhh. We are getting ready to tape."

Our trip to Nashville was very enjoyable. I will always remember getting a glimpse of a side of Jim I had never seen before.

The week Jim let his hair down in Music City.

The Speech Never Given

A few years ago, when my brother, Jack, was elected to the Clinton County Sports Hall of Fame, I prepared a speech should I be called upon to sponsor him at the induction banquet.

"Thank you ladies and gentlemen. It is indeed an honor to be asked to present to you my brother, Jack Haley, as a new member of the Clinton County Sports Hall of Fame. Also, please allow me to congratulate the other inductees who were also honored here tonight. It is a thrill to stand among so many Clinton County sports legends.

It is good to look out into the audience and see the faces of so many friends. It brings back so many fond memories. I presently live in Staunton Virginia, the home of the Statler Brothers. The Statler Brothers made famous a country song by the name of "Do You Remember These?" The Brothers ask in song if you remember, "duck tail hair, fender skirts, and peg in your pants?" I'm not a singer, but I'm going to ask you to sit back, relax, and remember with me as we look back up on the sports career of my brother, Jack Haley.

Jack was born and raised in Port William; a town of about one-hundred people. I hear some snickers, but name me another town in within Clinton County where such a large percentage of its population has been inducted into the Clinton County Sports Hall of Fame. Those of us who call Port home are very proud indeed of Jack Haley, Donnie Fields, Donnie DeVoe, Harold Reno, and the three Hoopers, Butch, Bobby and Vernon.

I was old enough and fortunate enough to have had the opportunity to see Jack in his prime. As a boy, Jack used to take me to the baseball diamond at Port to "hit some". Jack always liked to take a little infield and then hit some fly balls into the outfield. And hit them he did. The person that termed the phrase "major league pop-up" must have had Jack's fly balls in mind. The balls would go so high and stay up so long; well, I get dizzy just thinking about it.

The Haley Family of Port William produced many "firsts" on the baseball diamond and basketball court. Jack hit the first home run ever to go over the trees at Port William High School and land in Cap Mason's cornfield. Jim Haley, our brother, performed the first hidden ball trick during a varsity baseball game at Port. Jim was playing first base. The bases were loaded with two outs. Jim called time and trotted over to the pitcher's mound to have a few words with Jack. Jim moved back to his position and all of sudden reached over and tagged out the runner - saving another game for the Bulldogs. Jim had hidden the ball under his armpit.

Even Rita, our sister, had a first of sorts within the sports-minded Haley family. Rita bought Jack one of the first professional baseball gloves in Clinton County, one year before he left for spring training with the Cincinnati Reds. That glove cost $50.00. That was in the days when $50.00 really bought something.

I was privileged to witness the baseball that Jack hit over Rombach Avenue, in the air, against Wilmington High School. I know that was the first time such a shot ever occurred, and I'm not sure if it ever happened again.

One afternoon Jack was playing left field. I saw him throw-out a runner at home plate, who tried to score from second with a throw that never traveled more than a couple of feet off the ground. It was a laser. He threw a perfect strike from left field to the catcher, at a distance of almost 300 feet.

I also saw Jack break a window with a baseball he had hit at the old Lynchburg High School diamond. The school was at least 450 feet from home plate.

I was with Jack when his sports career took him to the old Clinton County Air Force Base, with the various softball teams from the area. Once when Jack was up to bat, I witnessed him bounce a softball off the windshield of the old "Flying Boxcars" that used to sit just a little too close to the ball diamond when Jack was playing.

I didn't get to go with Jack to Cincinnati's Crosley Field when the Reds signed him; but I remember him telling me how Frank McCormick, the Reds old first baseman, watched him warm up in the bullpen. Jack threw hard, extremely hard. It would have been nice to have had a radar gun back in those days.

Although Jack did not achieve his dream of playing in the Major Leagues, I am thoroughly convinced had he had the opportunity to play, he would have been very successful, for his ability surpassed many of those playing at the time. In fact, I believe he could easily have become a major league star once he became comfortable with his surroundings.

Gordy Coleman's words come to mind whenever I saw Jack threw a high hard one near the chin of a batter. Gordy would say that Jack had "sneaked into the kitchen and stole all his snacks." I saw more than one batter stand in place shaking, not ready to get back into the batters' box.

Dizzy Dean said the hardest ball he had ever seen hit "went through the pitcher's legs, and the center fielder caught it on the fly." Now that is a ball that is well hit. If anyone could ever hit a ball that hard, it was Jack.

I once heard an opposing player once remark that Jack Haley had one weakness. He was a nice man. He was not mean enough. If being nice is a weakness, then Jack must plead guilty. He not only was truly one of the nicest men to play sports in Clinton County, he is one of the nicest men in Clinton County. He was always a gentleman, a true gentle giant.

"Come on gang, let's rip," was Jack's battle cry. And do you know, most of the time the team would respond to Jack's exhortations, because they felt secure knowing if they got on base, Jack would certainly knock them home.

Jack was more than an outstanding athlete. He was a public

servant for 25 years as a police officer with the Wilmington Police Department. Jack is a family man, a God-fearing man.

A couple of years ago, I saw an article about Donnie DeVoe, a former Port William resident, in the Richmond, Virginia newspaper. The article talked about his new coaching job with Navy. I sent Don a short congratulatory note to express my best wishes for his successful season. A week later, I received a lovely, handwritten letter from Don. He thanked me for the article and for remembering him. He went on to say, how my note had reminded him of the many times he spent behind the Haley house after school playing basketball with Jack and the boys. He said he cherished those days, and that Jack Haley was his hero. Jack is my hero, too. Ladies and Gentlemen, I present Jack Haley.

The Unthinkable

Broadcast journalist Charlie Rose recently interviewed Robert Kennedy, Jr. as part of the observance of the 50th anniversary of the death of President John F. Kennedy. Kennedy told Rose he is convinced more than one gunman was responsible for the assassination of his uncle; and his father, Robert, never believed the Warren Commission Report.

Rose asked if his father, who was the U.S. attorney general at the time of his brother's death, felt there might have been a link between his very aggressive efforts against organized crime. "My father's investigators found phone records of Oswald and nightclub owner Jack Ruby, who killed Oswald two days after the president's assassination, filled with names of mafia leaders," Kennedy responded.

Kennedy's comments reminded me of an employee I met while serving as president of a biometric company in Nashville, Tennessee. We will call the individual Tony, an elderly man of smooth manner and an engaging personality.

One afternoon he came to my office to chat.

Tony said he began record promotions in Philadelphia with Myers Music Inc. In 1952, his boss, Jimmy Myers, a.k.a Jimmy De Knight, wrote the classic rock song, "Rock Around the Clock" with Max Freedman. "Years later, I came to Nashville as a record promoter for the group Alabama, and decided to stay, "Tony said.

"I was born on a very interesting street in Philadelphia. We lived at 13th and Mifflin Streets in South Philly. Some of my neighbors were noted singers from the 50's and 60's: Frankie Avalon, Chubby Checker, Fabian, Bobby Rydell, Al Martino, and Eddie Fisher. Several of us went to Southern High School together," Tony continued.

"Did they get you started in the music business?" I asked. Tony laughed and said, "No, not exactly." Tony said he had grown up with other interesting neighbors on Mifflin Street as well. He said he started first grade with Angelo Bruno, played street ball with Nicky Scarfo both who later became infamous gangsters. In fact, he said his mother and sister still lived on Mifflin Street. He said most of his friends were prominent members of the Philadelphia crime family, also known as the Scarfo crime family, Bruno crime family, or the Philly Mob.

"Oh," I said, not knowing how much more I wanted to know.

Tony went on to say that when he was in high school, a friend asked him to board a train and take a paper sack to another friend in New York City. Now, as Tony warmed-up, I sat forward in my chair, spellbound by the stories I was hearing.

He said he was glad to help a friend, but soon found they

wanted him to continue to drop-off bags. As time went on his area grew, and soon he was going to New Jersey, Boston, Cleveland, and Dallas. He said many of his stops included visits to radio stations and nightclubs. I was getting nervous now. I asked if this was when 'payola' became a national issue.

"It sure was," he said.

My first thought was this was an older man exaggerating stories. Then, he pulled some photographs from his briefcase. There was a photograph of Tony and a gangster. Then a newspaper photograph of a crime scene. You know the kind; a gangster lying on the street with bullet holes in his new suit. However, this one was different. The street sign in the picture read 13th Street and Mifflin Street. Tony was in his mother's front yard.

"It looks like you knew a lot of famous people," I said.

"I guess so. I even knew Jack Ruby, the man who shot Lee Harvey Oswald," Tony continued.

"How did you know Jack Ruby?" I asked. Tony said that in November 1963, a friend, Vicky Morosan, called him from Dallas, Texas. Vicky owned Band Box Records in Denver and Dallas at the time. Tony said Vicky told him she had just met a man named Jack Ruby who owned the Carousel Club also in Dallas.

According to Tony, Vicky had a new singer who wanted to cut a record and Ruby was promoting the new singer. Vicky said that Ruby was going to be calling Tony about promoting the singer's upcoming record. They would release it on Morosan's Band Box label.

Tony said on November 16, 1963, Jack Ruby did call him. Ruby wanted Tony to fly to Dallas in two weeks to sit in on the recording session. Ruby told Tony he had about $10,000.00 to make the recording, which was a lot of money in those days. Tony then said he had called Ruby back on November 19, 1963.

"A few days later, I was sitting with my mother and sister in Philadelphia watching the black-and-white TV coverage of the Kennedy assassination when I heard Don Rather say, "Watch the man in the hat."

Tony said he was horrified. He said he could not believe the shooter was Jack Ruby.

"Suddenly, the telephone rang. The caller was Vicky Morosan from Dallas," he said. "Did you see the shooting?" she asked. She was panicking, Tony recalled. Tony said he was just as scared as Vicky was because he knew his name and phone number was in Ruby's records. He said he never opened his mouth for years after the shooting because he still had many boyhood friends living in Philadelphia.

Tony said his boss, Jimmy Myers, gave him the name of an attorney. The attorney told Tony, "Do nothing and keep your mouth shut. When the FBI calls, tell them you have an attorney and have them call me immediately."

In 2006, forty-three years later, and no FBI investigator has ever contacted Tony. Were Oswald and Ruby two misguided killers or part of a conspiracy? We may never know for sure. It is truly the unthinkable.

Missiles in the Cornfields

We could see the worry in the faces of our parents. We did not eat much. None of us were hungry.

On Friday November 22, 1963, I was sitting in the old Wilmington Junior High study hall. Mrs. Elizabeth Camp interrupted the class to say Principal Myron Halley was on our school intercom for a very important news report.

A few seconds later, CBS reporter, Walter Cronkite, interrupted the broadcast of As the World Turns, and announced that rifle shots had struck President John F. Kennedy's motorcade in Dallas, Texas. A few minutes later, Mr. Cronkite returned to the air to say that those shots had fatally wounded the young president. The world was stunned.

It is hard to believe that forty-nine years have passed since that sad day in our history. This past month, October 16, 2012, marked the 50th anniversary of another significant event of the Kennedy Administration. The beginning of the Cuban Missile Crisis, days of fear and uncertainty that mercifully ended peacefully on October 28, 1962.

October is the best month of the year. The

weather is breathtaking, and our spirits soar as the leaves begin to turn, and Ohio changes into some of the most gorgeous scenery in the world.

Ohio State begins to march across the field in earnest, and our children and grandchildren become Superman, Flash, and Wonder Woman on Halloween.

At night, we sit around outdoor fires as the gentle autumn breeze bit by bit carries away the heat of summer, and delicately prepares us for the coming of the Ohio winter.

Not all Octobers have been peaceful and serene, however. It is only history to children and teenagers, but anyone in their mid-50s or older will remember the days of the crisis. To understand best the impact those twelve days had on America, one must look at the 1950's.

Some have described the 50's as an innocent time. Elvis appeared on the Ed Sullivan Show singing Hound Dog. Hula-hoops were popular, most loved Lucy, and Davy Crockett rode across America in a coonskin cap.

But, there was a fear, too. The fear of nuclear war was real.

Mr. Wiley Manker, Principal of Liberty Local School in Port William, showed us films that explained to grade school children how to survive a nuclear attack. One film, called *Duck and Cover*, taught us to kneel under our desks and to cover our heads with our arms. During recess, the occasional B52 bomber flew over Port William on its way back to Wright Patterson Air Force Base, reminding us of the dangers of the Cold War.

Then, one frightening day in mid-October 1962, there was suddenly real talk of nuclear warheads and missiles.

I had just come home from school. The front door opened and our mother said, "Pat, be quiet. This is important." With those words, she returned her attention to the old black and white Zenith TV. There were rumors of missiles in Cuba.

It was very unusual to see mom watching TV in the daytime so the news had to be important. Normally, at this time of day she was busy preparing dinner.

Our dad arrived home from work, and our family quietly sat down for dinner. These were the days when families shared meals together. Tonight was different for some reason. There was a noticeable degree of unease. We could see the worry in the faces of our parents. We did not eat much. None of us were hungry.

On October 22, 1962 at 7:00 p.m., then President John Kennedy delivered a special televised address to the nation, confirming the discovery of missiles in Cuba.

The news was staggering. The words spoken by the President echoed throughout our heads. "The policy of the United States was to regard any nuclear missile launched from Cuba against any nation in the Western Hemisphere as an attack by the Soviet Union on the United States, requiring a full retaliatory response upon the Soviet Union."

It is hard to describe the feelings of that moment. Fear began to creep over our home like a fog, blotting out reality.

President Kennedy went on to talk about intercepting Russian ships at sea, and invoking a 'quarantine' on any ships coming toward Cuba.

Our dad, who was never late for work, let alone prone to missing a day on the job, talked to us about staying home the following day. That added to our alarm. Our mother turned to my brother and me and said, "You two boys are not going to school tomorrow. You will stay home with me."

"Is there anywhere we can go?" I asked my mom.

"Nowhere," mom responded. "We are as safe at home as anyplace else."

She did not ask for my opinion, and none was offered. Our teachers had always told us that military installations would be the primary targets. Mrs. Gleason had given us that information thinking it would calm us. Now, it had the opposite effect. Clinton County was near Wright Patterson Air Force Base (home of the B52), the Wilmington Nike Center, and the Clinton County Air Force Base. We found ourselves within a triangle of danger.

A few months earlier, our family had taken a ride to see the new Nike Missile Base shrouded within the cornfields off Route 730. Surrounded by the acres of corn, suddenly it was easy to picture the doors of the missile silos opening and the ballistic missiles being primed for launch.

In our home, our parents remained calm. It kept our family grounded. "We are going to pray," my dad said.

With those simple words, he gave us a powerful message of hope. Within our faith, the lighting of candles is a tradition that has comforted many people through times of crisis. We lit three candles. We all knew, at such times, the candle is a beacon, a symbol of hope.

Thankfully, on Wednesday, October 24, 1962 at 10:25 a.m., the nation learned that President Kennedy had received a critical message. The Soviet ships were turning back.

Things have changed, of course, since 1962. However, Ohio is still the prettiest place on earth in October. The days are bright, the air is crisp, and the corn is ready for market. It is good to be alive in October.

Drinking from a Tin Cup at the Roadside Parks in Clinton County.

During one of visits to the park on a warm, late spring evening not too long ago, we sat in the swing

My wife, Brenda, and I were taking a walk recently at the J.W. Denver Williams Memorial Park in Wilmington, when we passed two or three large, white pillars lying in the brush alongside the walking trail.

Those pillars once stood in the middle of the park, holding together a bandstand where the Wilmington Municipal Band performed community concerts once a week. "Brenda, in a way, those pillars are symbolic now," I said as we continued down the path. "Those columns represented music festivals, fellowship and time spent with our friends and neighbors."

"Right over there was a large picnic shelter house with their large brick fireplaces," I continued. "We came here frequently for picnics, and would sit in the shade under that large tree there. When we were younger, we'd jump in the small wading pool that sat between the slides, swings and merry-go-around. My mother would fry potatoes and cook hamburgers on the open fire fueled by wood."

Years ago, Clinton County had a network of great roadside parks. The State-run parks were quaint, delightful places to visit. Cuba had a great location nestled in the triangle at 68 south and Cuba Road. Many times, we would be sitting at one of the picnic tables eating, when a train would pass by on its way to Wilmington and beyond.

The roadside park near New Vienna on South 73 was directly across from Snow Hill Country Club. Remnants of it still stand today. My brother, Kevin, and I were fascinated to read the names on the metal pad that hung from the side of the pump for travelers to sign, and most did. We loved to read the names and the towns they were from, and imagined them as they journeyed to their destinations.

The road to Cincinnati was at one time part of the present Clarksville Road. A park sat back just a little from State Route 22 and 3. It boasted picnic tables, a small shelter house, and a cool breeze that flowed beneath the large walnut shade trees that kept watch over the spot. The next time you drive on Clarksville Road, if you look closely you will see part of the drinking well and water pump in the shelter, still sitting in the front yard of a delightful home across from Adams School.

My favorite county park at this time was the one located just outside Martinsville on SR 28 between Martinsville and Midland. As time went by and the small, charming parks began to close, my parents and my family took one last ride to this park when we heard it was going to shut down. The meal that night was one of the best we had ever eaten, partly because we knew the next day workers were coming to dismantle the park. We were saddened to see it go.

Most of the small parks had a large pump in the middle of a gravel path that led to the picnic tables, and a small roof usually shaded the water pump. It is hard to believe today, but all of the visitors at the park drank from the same tin cup, held together by a small chain that hung from the top of the pump. There is no taste in the world like a drink of cold, clear, pure well water pumped by hand. No one thought a thing about it back then.

Brenda, and I still hold onto a little piece of those bygone days when we cookout at the little roadside park that remains near the corporation line of Blanchester located on 28 heading toward Goshen. "What would you like to eat?" Brenda will ask me, already anticipating my answer.

"Why don't we fry some potatoes and a couple of hamburgers," I respond with a smile and a nod to the past. After supper, we never fail to walk over to the large swing that faces the highway, sit down. and leisurely watch the traffic flow by.

During one of visits to the park on a warm, late spring evening not too long ago, we sat in the swing and talked about how today we are, in a sense, repeating the rituals of our parents and grandparents.

I often wonder if the people would still take the time to sign the registers.

The Clicking Clock in Richmond

Suddenly, the red phone rang. It startled me. It was the warden at the prison.

"It's said that truth and justice go hand in hand. Just ask Grady Finch, who thought he could cheat them both. Consider Grady's fate nothing more than a sentence deferred...in the Twilight Zone."

This quote was from an episode of the *Twilight Zone* some years ago. It begins with Grady Finch awaiting execution after the jury found him guilty of the murder of a convenience store owner.

In the cell, Grady insists to his lawyer, Liz, that he is innocent. The warden arrives and tells him that the governor has chosen not to issue a stay of execution. Grady is taken to the execution chamber. As they rig him with the tubes for lethal injection, Grady uses his final words to insist that he did not kill anyone. The executioner begins the injection process. The red phone rings and a member of the Governor's staff informs the warden and the executioner that there is a stay of execution.

Little did I know I would find myself in a

similar situation. Not as the condemned man, but as a staff member of Governor Jim Gilmore of Virginia, who assigned me the duty of staffing the phone in his office during an execution.

Governor Gilmore knew my background as a former sheriff, and requested I perform this duty. I reluctantly agreed.

The Attorney General of the Commonwealth of Virginia provided me with a very specific set of guidelines to follow during the time leading-up to the execution. I was admonished not to vary from the printed procedure.

On the night on the unpleasant assignment, the court had set the time of execution for 8:00 p.m. I was aware that the prisoner's attorney had appealed to the Supreme Court. There was always the possibility a stay of execution might be granted.

Suddenly, the red phone rang. It startled me. It was the warden at the prison. His calm tone and easy demeanor surprised me. He matter-of-factly reviewed the procedures the prison officials would be following prior to and during the execution, if it should, in fact, occur.

I glanced at my watch. It was 7:35 p.m. I began to perspire. I second-guessed myself for accepting this assignment. There was a real sense of gravity. I was the only one in the room, alone with a ticking clock.

As the clock ticked one minute after another, I wondered what was happening at the prison a few miles south of Richmond. What was going through the condemned man's mind? Would the red phone on the desk ring, commuting the sentence and sparing the man's life? On the other hand, would the minutes continue to pass as executioners began the process?

I became increasingly uneasy and restless. I wanted to pace the floor, but I could not. I had to stay beside the phone. The convicted man's life depended upon it.

It was 7:48 p.m. and the phone has remained eerily silent. The plight of the condemned man lay in the balance of a few minutes.

At was exactly 7:59 p.m. The red phone rang. It was the Governor. There was a stay of execution.

The ticking clock almost seemed to stop. I got-up from my chair, determined never to sit there again.

About the Author

Pat Haley lives in Clinton County, a mere six miles from the home in Port William, Ohio, where he was born and raised by his parents, Bob and Ellen. Much of his writing draws on the appreciation of stories and experiences he has encountered during his travels through life, and his interactions with friends and family.

Pat is the bestselling author of *The Danes Murders: Lost Innocence in Lees Creek*. The book is a personal account of the investigation into the tragic murders of several members of a well-loved family in the small farming community within Clinton County.

Pat currently writes a weekly human interest column for the local newspaper, the Wilmington News Journal.

He and his family love sports, particularly baseball. Pat hit the first two home runs ever hit on the Pony Baseball Diamond at J.W. Denver Williams Jr. Memorial Park in 1963. Both were hit to deep right center on fastballs high and tight.

Pat served his community as the county sheriff for many years, and presently is in his first term as county commissioner.

He and his wife, Brenda, lived in the Shenandoah Valley of Virginia for twelve years returning to their home area of Clinton County in 2007. Son, daughter-in-law and grandson—Greg, Kristen and Jack—live in Lexington, Kentucky.